ISLAM AND THE CHALLENGE OF DEMOCRACY

ISLAM

AND THE

CHALLENGE
OF DEMOCRACY

A   B O S T O N   R E V I E W   B O O K

Khaled Abou El Fadl

EDITED BY

JOSHUA COHEN

AND DEBORAH CHASMAN

PRINCETON UNIVERSITY PRESS ▨ *Princeton and Oxford*

LIBRARY OF CONGRESS CATALOGING-IN-PUBLICATION DATA

Abou El Fadl, Khaled, 1963–
Islam and the challenge of democracy / Khaled Abou El Fadl ; edited
by Joshua Cohen and Deborah Chasman.
p.   cm.
Includes bibliographical references and index.
ISBN 0-691-11841-8 (cl : alk. paper)—ISBN 0-691-11938-4 (pb : alk. paper)
1. Islam and politics.   2. Religion and politics—Islamic countries.
3. Democracy—Religious aspects—Islam.   4. Islam—21st century.
I. Cohen, Joshua, 1951–   II. Chasman, Deborah.   III. Title.

BP 173.7.A264 2004
297.2'72—dc22   2003062311

British Library Cataloging-in-Publication Data is available

This book has been composed in Garamond Book

Printed on acid free-paper. ⊜

www.pupress.princeton.edu

Printed in the United States of America

3   5   7   9   10   8   6   4

ISBN-13: 978-0-691-11938-0 (pbk.)

CONTENTS

Islam and the Challenge of Democracy

KHALED ABOU EL FADL

◈ A Muslim jurist writing a few centuries ago on the subject of Islam and government would have commenced his treatise by distinguishing three types of political systems. The first he would have described as a natural system—like a primitive state of nature, an uncivilized, anarchic world where the most powerful tyrannize the rest. Instead of law there would be custom; instead of government there would be tribal elders who would be obeyed only so long as they remained the strongest.

The jurist would then describe a second system, ruled by a prince or king whose word is the law. Because the law would be fixed by the arbitrary will of the ruler and the people would obey out of necessity or compulsion, this system, too, would be tyrannical and illegitimate.

The third and best system would be the caliphate, based on Shari'ah law—the body of Muslim religious law founded on the Qur'an and the conduct and statements of the Prophet. According to Muslim jurists, Shari'ah law fulfills the criteria of justice and legitimacy and binds the governed and governor alike. Because it is based on the rule of law and thus deprives human beings of arbitrary authority over each other, the caliphate system was considered superior to any other.[1]

In espousing the rule of law and limited government, classical Muslim scholars embraced core elements of modern democratic practice. Limited government and the rule of law, however, are only two elements in the system of government with the most compelling claim to legitimacy today. Democracy's moral power lies in the idea that the citizens of a nation are sovereign, and—in modern representative democracies—they express their sovereign will by electing representatives. In a democracy, the people are the source of the law, and the law in turn ensures the fundamental rights that protect the well-being and interests of the individual members of the sovereignty.

For Islam, democracy poses a formidable challenge. Muslim jurists have argued that law made by a sovereign monarch is illegitimate because it substitutes human authority for God's sovereignty. But law made by sovereign citizens faces the same problem of legitimacy. In Islam, God is the only sovereign and the ultimate source of legitimate law. How, then, can a democratic conception of the people's authority be reconciled with an Islamic understanding of God's authority?

Answering this question is extraordinarily important but also extraordinarily difficult, for both political and conceptual reasons. On the political side, democracy faces a number of practical hurdles in Islamic countries—authoritarian political traditions, a history of colonial and imperial rule, and state domination of the economy and society. But philosophical and doctrinal questions are important too, and I propose to focus on them here as the beginning of a discussion of the possibilities for democracy in the Islamic world.

A central conceptual problem is that modern democracy evolved over centuries within the distinctive context of a post-Reformation, market-oriented Christian Europe. Does it make sense to look for points of contact in a remarkably different context? My answer begins from the premise that democracy and Islam are defined in the first instance by their underlying moral values and the attitudinal commitments of their adherents—not by the ways that those values and commitments have been applied. If we focus on those fundamental moral values, we will see that the tradition of Islamic political thought contains both interpretive and practical possibilities that can be developed into a democratic system. To be sure, these doctrinal potentialities may remain unrealized: without willpower, an inspired vision, and a moral commitment there can be no democracy in Islam. But Muslims, for whom Islam is the authoritative frame of reference, can arrive at the conviction that democracy is an ethical good, and that the pursuit of this good does not require abandoning Islam.

DEMOCRACY AND DIVINE SOVEREIGNTY

Although Muslim jurists debated political systems, the Qur'an itself does not specify a particular form of government. But it does identify a set of social and political values that are central to a Muslim polity. Three values are of particular importance: pursuing justice through social cooperation and mutual assistance (49:13, 11:119); establishing a nonautocratic, consultative method of governance; and institutionalizing mercy and compassion in social interactions (6:12, 6:54, 21:107, 27:77, 29:51, 45:20). So, all else being equal, Muslims today ought to endorse the form of government that is most effective in helping them promote these values.

The Case for Democracy

Several considerations suggest that democracy—and especially a constitutional democracy that protects basic individual rights—is that form. My central argument (others will emerge later) is that democracy—by assigning equal rights of speech, association, and suffrage to all—offers the greatest potential for promoting justice and protecting human dignity, without making God responsible for injustice or the degradation of human beings. A fundamental Qur'anic idea is that God vested all of humanity with a kind of divinity by making every person the viceroy of God on this earth: "Remember, when your Lord said to the angels: 'I have to place a vicegerent on earth,' they said: 'Will you place one there who will create disorder and shed blood, while we intone Your litanies and sanctify Your name?' And God said: 'I know what you do not know'" (2:30). In particular, human beings, as God's vicegerents, are responsible for making the world more just. By assigning equal political rights to all adults, democracy expresses that special status of human beings in God's creation and enables them to discharge that responsibility.

Of course, God's vicegerent does not share God's perfection of judgment and will. A constitutional democracy, then, acknowledges the errors of judgment, temptations, and vices associated with human fallibility by enshrining some basic moral standards in a constitutional document—moral standards that express the dignity of individuals. To be sure, democracy does not ensure justice. But it does establish a basis for pursuing justice and thus for fulfilling a fundamental responsibility assigned by God to each one of us.

In a representative democracy some individuals have greater authority than others. But a democratic system makes those authorities accountable to all and thus resists the tendency of the powerful to render themselves immune from judgment. This requirement of accountability is consistent with the imperative of justice in Islam. If a political system has no institutional mechanisms to call the unjust to account, then the system itself is unjust, regardless of whether injustice has actually been committed. If criminal law does not assign punishment for rape, then it is unjust, quite apart from whether that crime was ever committed. It is a moral good in and of itself that a democracy, through the institutions of the vote, the separation and division of power, and the guarantee of pluralism at least offers the possibility of redress.

We have a provisional case for democracy, then, founded on a fundamental Islamic idea about the special status of human beings in God's creation. It is provisional because we have not yet considered the great challenge to that case: how can the higher law of Shari'ah, founded on God's sovereignty, be reconciled with the democratic idea that the people, as the sovereign, can be free to flout Shari'ah law?

God as the Sovereign

Early in Islamic history the issue of God's political dominion (*hakimiyyat Allah*) was raised by a group known as the Haruriyya (later known as the Khawarij) when they rebelled against the fourth Rightly Guided Caliph 'Ali Ibn Abi Talib. Initially the supporters of 'Ali, the Haruriyya turned against him when he agreed to arbitrate his political dispute with a competing political faction, which was led by a man named Mu'awiya.

'Ali himself had agreed to the arbitration on the condition that the arbitrators be bound by the Qur'an and give full consideration to the supremacy of the Shari'ah. But the Khawarij—pious, puritanical, and fanatical—believed that God's law clearly supported 'Ali. So they rejected arbitration as inherently unlawful and, in effect, a challenge to God's sovereignty. According to the Khawarij, 'Ali's behavior showed that he was willing to compromise God's supremacy by transferring decision making to human agency. They declared 'Ali a traitor to God, and after efforts to reach a peaceful resolution failed, they assassinated him. After 'Ali's death,

Mu'awiya seized power and established himself as the first caliph
of the Umayyad Dynasty.

Anecdotal reports about the debates between 'Ali and the
Khawarij reflect unmistakable tension about the meaning of legality and the implications of the rule of law. In one such report
members of the Khawarij accused 'Ali of accepting the judgment
and dominion (*hakimiyya*) of human beings instead of abiding
by the dominion of God's law. Upon hearing of this accusation,
'Ali called on the people to gather around him and brought out a
large copy of the Qur'an. 'Ali touched the Qur'an while instructing it to speak to the people and inform them about God's law.
Surprised, the people who had gathered around 'Ali exclaimed,
"What are you doing? The Qur'an cannot speak, for it is not a
human being!" Upon hearing this, 'Ali exclaimed that this was exactly his point. The Qur'an, 'Ali explained, is but ink and paper,
and it does not speak for itself. Instead, it is human beings who
give effect to it according to their limited personal judgments and
opinions.[2]

Such stories are subject to multiple interpretations, but this one
points most importantly to the dogmatic superficiality of proclamations of God's sovereignty that sanctify human determinations.
Notably, the Khawarij's rallying cry of "Dominion belongs to God"
or "The Qur'an is the judge" (*la hukma illa li'llah* or *al-hukmu
li'l-Qur'an*) is nearly identical to the slogans invoked by contemporary fundamentalist groups.[3] But considering the historical
context, the Khawarij's sloganeering was initially a call for the
symbolism of legality and the supremacy of law that later de-
scended into an unequivocal radicalized demand for fixed lines of
demarcation between what is lawful and unlawful.

To a believer, God is all-powerful and the ultimate owner of the
heavens and earth. But when it comes to the laws in a political sys-

tem, arguments claiming that God is the sole legislator endorse a fatal fiction that is indefensible from the point of view of Islamic theology. Such arguments pretend that some human agents have perfect access to God's will, and that human beings could become the perfect executors of the divine will without inserting their own human judgments and inclinations in the process.

Moreover, claims about God's sovereignty assume that the divine legislative will seeks to regulate all human interactions, that Shari'ah is a complete moral code that prescribes for every eventuality. But perhaps God does not seek to regulate all human affairs, and instead leaves human beings considerable latitude in regulating their own affairs as long as they observe certain minimal standards of moral conduct, including the preservation and promotion of human dignity and well-being. In the Qur'anic discourse, God commanded creation to honor human beings because of the miracle of the human intellect—an expression of the abilities of the divine. Arguably, the fact that God honored the miracle of the human intellect and the human being as a symbol of divinity is sufficient to justify a moral commitment to protecting and preserving the integrity and dignity of that symbol of divinity. But—and this is 'Ali's central point—God's sovereignty provides no escape from the burdens of human agency.[4]

When human beings search for ways to approximate God's beauty and justice, then, they do not deny God's sovereignty; they honor it. They also honor it in the attempt to safeguard the moral values that reflect the attributes of the divine. If we say that the only legitimate source of law is the divine text and that human experience and intellect are irrelevant to the pursuit of the divine will, then divine sovereignty will always stand as an instrument of authoritarianism and an obstacle to democracy.[5] But that authoritarian view denigrates God's sovereignty.

I develop this argument later, but to make the case more compelling and accessible, I first lay a broader foundation for Islamic political and legal doctrines.

GOVERNMENT AND LAW

If, as many Muslim fundamentalists and Western Orientalists contend, God's dominion or sovereignty means that God is the sole legislator, then one would expect a caliph or Muslim ruler to be treated as God's agent or representative. If within a political system God is the only sovereign, then the ruler ought to be appointed by the divine sovereign, serve at His pleasure, and implement His will. But just as the meaning and implications of God's sovereignty were the subject of an intense debate in premodern Islam, so were the powers of the ruler and the place of law in circumscribing those powers. And some lines of argument in the debate resonate with modern democratic ideas.

Ruler and Ruled

It is well established, at least in Sunni Islam, that the Prophet died without naming a successor to lead the Muslim community. The Prophet intentionally left the choice of leadership to the Muslim nation as a whole.[6] A statement attributed to the Rightly Guided Caliph Abu Bakr asserts, "God has left people to manage their own affairs so that they will choose a leader who will serve their interests."[7]

The word *khalifa* (caliph), the title given to the Muslim leader, literally means successor or deputy. Early on Muslims debated whether it was appropriate to name the leader the Caliph of God (*khalifat Allah*), but most scholars preferred the designation Caliph of the Prophet of God (*khalifat rasul Allah*). But the Caliph—whether the Prophet's successor or God's deputy—did not enjoy the authority of either the Prophet or God, whose powers of legislation, revelation, absolution, and punishment cannot be delegated to any other. But how much of the Prophet's authority does the Caliph enjoy? And to whom does the Caliph answer?

If the Caliph's primary obligation is to implement divine law, then arguably the Caliph answers only to God. So long as the Caliph's actions are plausible interpretations of God's mandates, such interpretations must be accepted and the Caliph has fulfilled his duties to the people. Only God can assess the Caliph's intentions, and—most Sunni jurists argued—a ruler is not removable from power unless he commits a clear, visible, and major infraction against God (that is, a major sin).

Muslim jurists did not, however, completely sever the connection between the ruler and the people. In Sunni theory the caliphate must be based on an *'aqd* (a contract) between the Caliph and *ahl al-hall wa al-'aqd* (the people who have the power of contract), who give their *bay'a* (allegiance or consent to the Caliph): the Caliph is to receive the *bay'a* in return for his promise to discharge the terms of the contract. The terms of the contract were not extensively discussed in Islamic sources. Typically, jurists would include the obligation to apply God's law and to protect Muslims and the territory of Islam; in return, the ruler was promised the people's support and obedience. The assumption was that Shari'ah law defines the terms of the contract.

Who are the people that have the power to choose and remove the ruler? The Mu'tazili scholar[8] Abu Bakr al-Asam (d. A.H. 200 / A.D. 816) argued that the public at large must have this power: there must be a general consensus over the ruler, and each person must individually give his consent.[9] The vast majority of Muslim jurists argued more pragmatically that ahl al-hall wa al-ʿaqd are those who possess the necessary *shawka* (power or strength) to ensure the obedience or, in the alternative, the consent of the public.

The idea of the consent of the governed, despite its democratic resonance, ought not to be equated with conceptions of delegated powers or government by the people. Consent in premodern Muslim discourses appears to be the equivalent of acquiescence. Underlying these discussions is a certain amount of distrust toward the laity (*al-ʿamma*): "They [the laity] tend to float with every ebb and flow, and maybe [they] will be more content with choosing [to the caliphate] the wrongdoers instead of the righteous [rulers]."[10] This type of attitude was widespread among Muslim jurists, and considering the historical period in which they wrote—well before they had any experience with mass democracy or broad literacy—it is not surprising. As a result, many of the concepts employed in political discourses suggest an idea of representative government but never fully endorse it. In the dominant paradigm, both ruler and ruled are God's agents (*khulafa' Allah*) in implementing the divine law.

The Rule of Law

As noted earlier, an essential characteristic of a legitimate Islamic government is that it is subject to and limited by Shariʿah law. Although this concept does offer support for the rule of law, we must distinguish between the supremacy of law and the supremacy of a set of legal rules. The two are quite distinct, and both are suggested in the Islamic legal tradition. Once again, Islamic political thought contains a range of interpretive possibilities. And once again, some of these possibilities resonate more strongly with democratic principles.

In asserting the supremacy of Shari'ah, Muslim scholars typically argued that its positive commandments, such as punishment for adultery or for drinking alcohol, ought to be honored by the government. But a government that declares its intention to abide by all the positive commandments of Shari'ah may nevertheless manipulate the rules in order to obtain desired results. Under the pretense of guarding public modesty, the government could pass arbitrary laws forbidding many forms of public assembly; under the guise of protecting orthodoxy, it could pass arbitrary laws to punish creative expression; under the guise of protecting individuals from slander, it could suppress many forms of political and social criticism; and it could imprison or execute political dissenters, claiming that they are sowing *fitna* (discord and social turmoil). Arguably, all these governmental actions are Shari'ah-compliant unless there is a clear sense of the limits imposed on the ability of the government to service and promote even Shari'ah.

But the rule of law need not be taken to mean that the government is bound by a codebook of specific regulations. Instead, it might be interpreted as requiring a government to be bound by processes of making and interpreting laws, and even more important, as requiring that those processes themselves be bound by fundamental moral commitments—in particular to human dignity and freedom.

We find some evidence for this alternative conception of the rule of law in the premodern juristic literature. Jurists discussed the limits to be placed on the lawmaking power of the state, in part under the rubric of public interest (*al-masalih al-mursalah*) and blocking the means to illegality (*sadd al-dhari'ah*). Both jurisprudential concepts enabled the state to extend its lawmaking powers to fulfill a good or avoid an evil. For instance, pursuant to the principle of blocking the means, the lawmaker could claim that behavior that is lawful ought to be considered unlawful because it leads to the commission of illegal acts. In essence, both public interest and blocking the means made law more flexible and adaptive. Of course, they could be employed to expand the law not only in the service of the public good but at the expense of individual autonomy as well. In particular, blocking the means to evil, founded on the idea of preventive or precautionary measures (*al-ihtiyat*), could be exploited to expand the power of the state under the guise of protecting Shariʿah. This type of dynamic can be avoided in part by adopting procedural guarantees, but more important by understanding that the rule of law is about ensuring the dignity and freedoms of human beings, which Shariʿah can be utilized to justify but not to undermine.

An important dimension to the challenge of establishing the rule of law is the complex relationship between Shariʿah law, as articulated by jurists, and the administrative practices of the state or expediency laws (*al-ahkam al-siyasiyyah*). In the first two centuries of Islam it was possible to find jurists citing the practices of the state as a normative precedent, but this became increasingly rare. By the fourth/tenth century, Muslim jurists had established themselves as the only legitimate authority empowered to expound the law of God. The practice of the state was not considered illegitimate, but only the Muslim jurists could settle the law. The state was expected to enforce divine laws, not to determine their content.

Still, as the enforcer of divine laws, the state was granted broad discretion over matters of public interest (known as the field of *al-siyasah al-Sharʿiyyah*). State regulations were lawful and enforceable as long as they did not contravene the divine law—as expounded by the jurists—or constitute an abusive use of discre-

tion (*al-ta'assuf fi masa'il al-khiyar*). For this reason jurisprudential works meticulously documented the determinations of jurists but not state regulations, which were documented by state
functionaries in works on the administrative practices of the
state. In the dictum of Muslim jurists, Shari'ah is considered the
foundation of law, and politics is its protector. (Similarly, Muslim
jurists often assert that religion is the foundation and political authorities are its protector.)[11] This paradigm, however, leaves unre-
solved the core problem of how to clearly delineate the limits of
government power. To what extent can the government extend
the reach of its laws under the guise of guarding or properly fulfilling the purposes of Shari'ah?

Concerns about the reach of the government's power under
Shari'ah have antecedents in Islamic history, and so, by the standards of the modern age, this is not an entirely novel issue. But such
concerns are nearly absent from the framework of contemporary
Islamists. To date, Islamist models, whether in Iran, Saudi Arabia, or
Pakistan, have endowed the state with legislative power over the divine law. For instance, the claim of precautionary measures (blocking the means) is used in Saudi Arabia to justify a wide range of
restrictive laws against women, including the prohibition against
driving cars.[12] This is a relatively novel invention in Islamic state
practices and in many instances amounts to the use of Shari'ah to
undermine Shari'ah. The intrusive modern state invokes Shari'ah in
passing laws that create an oppressive condition—a condition that
itself is contrary to the principles of justice under Shari'ah.

Traditionally, Muslim jurists insisted that rulers ought to consult with jurists on all matters related to law, but the jurists themselves never demanded the right to rule the Islamic state directly.
In fact, until recently neither Sunni nor Shi'i jurists ever assumed
direct rule in the political sphere.[13] Throughout Islamic history,

the jurists (ulema) performed a wide range of economic, political, and administrative functions and, most important, acted as negotiatory mediators between the ruling classes and the laity. As Afaf Marsot states, "[The ulema] were the purveyors of Islam, the guardians of its tradition, the depository of ancestral wisdom, and the moral tutors of the population."[14] While they legitimated and often explained the rulers to the ruled, the jurists also used their moral weight to thwart tyrannous measures and at times led or legitimated rebellions against the ruling classes. Modernity, however, has turned the ulema from "vociferous spokesmen of the masses" into salaried state functionaries who play a primarily conservative, legitimist role for the ruling regimes in the Islamic world.[15] The disintegration of the role of the ulema and their cooptation by the modern praetorian state, with its hybrid practices of secularism, have opened the door for the state to become the maker and enforcer of the divine law; in so doing the state has acquired formidable power, which has further ingrained the practice of authoritarianism in various Islamic states.

Consultative Government

The Qur'an instructs the Prophet to consult regularly with Muslims on all significant matters and indicates that a society that conducts its affairs through some form of deliberative process is considered praiseworthy in the eyes of God (3:159, 42:38). There are many historical reports suggesting that the Prophet consulted regularly with his Companions regarding the affairs of the state.[16] In addition, shortly after the death of the Prophet, the concept of *shura* (consultative deliberations) had become a symbol signifying participatory politics and legitimacy. The failure to enforce or adhere to shura became a common theme invoked in narratives of oppression and rebellion. For example, it is reported that the Prophet's cousin ʿAli reproached Umar b. al-Khattab, the second caliph, and Abu Bakr, the first caliph, for not respecting the shura by nominating Abu Bakr to the caliphate in the absence of the Prophet's family. And the opposition to ʿUthman b. ʿAffan (r. 23–35/644–656), the third Rightly Guided Caliph, accused him of destroying the rule of shura because of his alleged nepotistic and autocratic policies.[17]

Although the precise meaning of *shura* in these historical narratives is unclear, the concept most certainly did not refer merely to a ruler's solicitation of opinions from notables in society; it signified, more broadly, resistance to autocracy, government by force, or oppression. This is consistent with the juristic hostility toward despotism (*al-istibdad*) and whimsical and autocratic governance (*al-hukm bi'l hawa wa al-tasallut*). Even when Muslim jurists prohibited rebellions against despotic rulers, they tolerated despotism as a necessary evil, not as a desirable good.

After the third/ninth century, the concept of shura took more concrete institutional shape in the discourses of Muslim jurists. Shura became the formal act of consulting *ahl al-shura* (the people of consultation), who according to the juristic sources were the same group of people who constituted *ahl al-ʿaqd* (the people who choose the ruler). Sunni jurists debated whether the results of the consultative process were binding (*shura mulzima*) or nonbinding (*ghayr mulzima*). If the shura is binding, then the ruler must abide by the determinations made by ahl al-shura. The majority of jurists, however, concluded that the determinations of ahl al-shura were advisory and not compulsory. But—rather inconsistently—many jurists asserted that after consultation, the ruler must follow the opinion that is most consistent with the Qur'an, the Sunna, and the consensus of jurists. Al-Ghazali expressed the general consensus when he said that "[d]espotic, nonconsultative, decision making, even if from a wise and learned person, is objectionable and unacceptable."[18]

Modern reformists have seized upon the ideal of a consultative government as a way of arguing for the basic compatibility between Islam and democracy. But even if the ethic of shura is expanded into a broader concept of participatory government, concerns about majority tyranny underscore that the moral commitments informing the lawmaking process are as important as the process itself. So even if shura is transformed into an instrument of participatory representation, it must be limited by a scheme of private and individual rights that serve an overriding moral goal such as justice. In other words, shura must be valued not because of the results it produces but because it represents a moral value in itself. Consequently, regardless of the value of specific dissenting views, dissent would be tolerated because doing so would be seen as a basic part of the mandate of justice.

The Islamic tradition of legal-political thought, then, suggests ideas of representation, consultation, and legal process. But the precise content of these ideas remains contested and provides no direct link between Islam and democracy. To understand the democratic possibilities of Islam, we must look more deeply into the role of human beings in God's creation and the central importance of justice in human life assigned by the Qur'an.

JUSTICE AND MERCY

Justice plays a central role in the Qur'anic discourse; it is an obligation we owe to God and to one another. In addition, the imperative of justice is tied to the obligations of enjoining the good and forbidding the evil and the necessity of bearing witness on God's behalf. Even though the Qur'an does not define the constituent elements of justice, it emphasizes the ability to achieve justice as a unique human charge and necessity—an obligation that falls on all of us in our capacity as vicegerents.[19] In essence, the Qur'an requires a commitment to a moral imperative that is vague but recognizable through intuition, reason, and human experience.

The Islamic debate about how government might serve justice is remarkably similar to seventeenth-century Western discourse on the state of nature or the original condition of human beings. One view—advanced by Ibn Khaldun and al-Ghazali—argued that human beings are by nature fractious, contentious, and not inclined toward cooperation. So, government is necessary to force people, contrary to their natures, to cooperate with each other and to promote justice and the general interest.

Another school of thought, exemplified by al-Mawardi and Ibn Abi al-Rabi', argued that God created human beings weak and in need so that they would cooperate by necessity; this cooperation would limit injustice by restraining the strong and safeguarding the rights of the weak. Furthermore, God created human beings different from one another so that they would need each other to achieve their aims. In this school of thought, human beings by nature desire justice and tend to cooperate in order to achieve it. Even if human beings exploit the divine gift of intellect and the guidance of the law of God, through cooperation they are bound to reach a greater level of justice and moral fulfillment. And the ruler ascends to power through a contract with the people, pursuant to which he undertakes to further the cooperation of the people with the ultimate goal of achieving a just society.

In reflecting on the demands of justice, the juristic argument about human diversity and cooperation is especially important. The Qur'an states that God created people different and grouped them into nations and tribes so that they would come to know one another. Muslim jurists reasoned that the expression "come to know one another" indicates the need for social cooperation and mutual assistance in order to achieve justice (49:13). The Qur'an also notes that people will remain different from one another until the end of human existence and that the reality of human diversity is part of the divine wisdom and an intentional purpose of creation: "If thy Lord had so willed, He could have made mankind one people, but they will not cease to dispute" (11:118).

The Qur'anic celebration and sanctification of human diversity incorporates that diversity into the purposeful pursuit of justice and creates various possibilities for a pluralistic commitment in modern Islam. That commitment could be developed into an ethic that respects dissent and honors the right of human beings to be different, including the right to adhere to different religious or nonreligious convictions. At the political level it could be appropriated into a normative stance that considers justice and diversity as core values that a democratic constitutional order is bound to protect. Furthermore, it could be developed into a notion of delegated powers, in which the ruler is entrusted with serving the core value of justice by ensuring the rights of assembly, cooperation, and dissent. Even more, a notion of limits could be developed that would restrain the government from derailing the quest for justice or from hampering the right of the people to cooperate, or dissent, in this quest. Importantly, if the government failed to discharge the obligations of its covenant, it would lose its legitimate claim to power.

Unfortunately, several factors militate against the fulfillment of these possibilities in modern Islam. At the theological and philosophical level, the constituents of justice have not been subjected to a close examination in Islamic doctrine. And part of the explanation for that limitation lies in a basic tension in understanding the nature of justice. Does the divine law define justice, or does justice define the divine law? If the former, then whatever one concludes is the divine law therein is justice. If the latter, then whatever justice demands is, in fact, the demand of the divine.

If we can know what justice requires by first determining what the divine law is, then there is no point in investigating the demands of justice—whether justice means equality of opportunities or of results, fostering personal autonomy, maximizing collective utility, or guarding basic human dignity. If the divine law is prior to justice, then the just society is no longer about rights of speech and assembly or the right to explore the means to justice, but simply about the implementation of the divine law.

Suppose instead that we accept the primacy of justice in the Qur'anic discourse, the notion of human vicegerency, and the idea that the duty to foster justice has been assigned to humanity at large. A reasonable conclusion would be that the value of justice ought to control and guide all efforts at interpreting and understanding divine law. This requires a serious paradigm shift in Islamic thinking. In my view, justice is a divine imperative and represents the sovereignty of the divine. God describes God's self as inherently just, and the Qur'an asserts that God has decreed mercy upon God's self (6:12, 54). Furthermore, the very purpose of entrusting the divine message to the Prophet Muhammad was a gift of mercy to human beings.[20]

In the Qur'anic discourse, mercy is not simply forgiveness; nor is it the willingness to ignore the faults and sins of people.[21] Rather it is a state in which the individual is able to be just with him- or herself and others by giving each individual person his or her due. Fundamentally, mercy is tied to a state of genuine

perception of others—which is why in the Qur'an mercy is coupled with the need for human beings to be patient with and tolerant of each other.[22] Most significantly, diversity and differences
among human beings are claimed in the Qur'anic discourse to be
merciful divine gifts to humankind (11:119).[23] Genuine perception that enables people to understand, appreciate, and become
enriched by the diversity of humanity is one of the constituent elements for founding a just society and achieving justice. The divine charge to human beings at large and Muslims in particular is,
as the Qur'an puts it, "to know one another" and to utilize this
genuine knowledge in an effort to pursue justice.

On this view, then, the divine mandate for a Muslim polity is to
pursue justice by adhering to the need for mercy. Although
coexistence is a basic necessity for mercy, in order to pursue genuine knowledge of the other and aspire to a state of justice human
beings need to cooperate in seeking the good and the beautiful,
and do so by engaging in a purposeful moral discourse. Implementing legalistic rules, even if such rules are the product of an
interpretation of divine texts, is not sufficient for mercy—genuine
perception of the other—or, ultimately, for justice.

So principles of mercy and justice are the primary divine
charge, and God's sovereignty lies in the fact that God is the authority that delegated to human beings the task of achieving justice on earth by fulfilling the virtues that approximate divinity.[24]
This conception of divine sovereignty does not negate human
agency by requiring a mechanical enforcement of rules; instead, it
accommodates our agency and even promotes it insofar as it con-
tributes to the fulfillment of justice. Significantly, according to the
juristic discourses, it is not possible to achieve justice unless
every possessor of a right (*haqq*) is granted his or her right. The
challenge for human vicegerents is to recognize that a right exists,

to understand who is the possessor of such a right, and ultimately to ensure that the possessor enjoys the right. A society that fails in this task—no matter how many rules it applies—is neither merciful nor just. This places us in a position to explore the possibility of individual rights in Islam.

INDIVIDUAL RIGHTS

All constitutional democracies afford strong protections to certain individual interests through rights of free speech and assembly, equality before the law, rights to property, and guarantees of due process. But which rights ought to be protected, and to what extent, is subject to a large measure of variation in theory and practice. Here I will suppose that whatever the precise nature of rights, some individual interests ought to be treated as unassailable. These unassailable interests are those whose violation communicates to the individual in question a sense of worthlessness and tends to destroy the faculty of a human being to comprehend the necessary elements for a dignified existence. So, use of torture and denial of food, shelter, or means of sustenance, such as employment, are always unacceptable.

To understand the traditional place of protected interests in Islamic law it is important to note that the purpose of Shari'ah in jurisprudential theory is to ensure the welfare of the people (*tahqiq masalih al-'ibad*). Typically, Muslim jurists divided the welfare of the people into three categories: necessities (*daruriyyat*), needs (*hajiyyat*), and luxuries (*kamaliyyat* or *tahsiniyyat*). According to Muslim jurists, the law and policies of the government must fulfill these interests, in descending order of importance—first necessities, then needs, then luxuries. The necessities are further divided into five basic values—*al-daruriyyat al-khamsah*: religion,

life, intellect, lineage or honor, and property.[25] But Muslim jurists
did not develop the five basic values as broad categories and then
explore the theoretical implications of each value. Rather, in a
positivistic spirit, they examined existing legal injunctions that
could be said to serve each of the values and concluded that
by codifiying each of these specific injunctions, the five values
would be sufficiently served. So, for example, Muslim jurists con-
tended that the law of apostasy protected religion, the prohibition of murder served the basic value of life, the prohibition of
intoxicants protected the intellect, the prohibition of fornication
and adultery protected lineage, and the right of compensation
protected the right to property.[26] But limiting the protection of
the intellect to the prohibition of alcohol or the protection of life
to the prohibition of murder is hardly thorough. Unfortunately, it
appears that the juristic tradition reduced these five values to
technical objectives. Still, the broad values asserted could serve as
a foundation for a systematic theory of individual rights in the
modern age.[27]

To be sure, the juristic tradition articulated a wealth of positions
that exhibit an orientation toward protections for individuals. For
instance, Muslim jurists developed the idea of presumption of in-
nocence in criminal and civil proceedings and argued that the
accuser always carries the burden of proof (*al-bayyina ʿala man
iddaʿa*). In matters related to heresy, Muslim jurists repeatedly argued that it is better to let a thousand heretics go free than to
wrongfully punish a single sincere Muslim. In criminal cases the jurists argued that it is always better to release a guilty person than
to run the risk of punishing an innocent one.[28] Moreover, many jurists condemned the practice of detaining or incarcerating hetero-
dox groups even when such groups openly advocated and
proselytized their heterodoxy (such as the Khawarij), and they ar-

gued that such groups may not be harassed or molested until they carry arms and form a clear intent to rebel against the government.[29] Muslim jurists also condemned the use of torture, arguing that the Prophet forbade the use of *muthla* (mutilations) in all situations,[30] and they opposed the use of coerced confessions in all legal and political matters.[31] In fact, a large number of jurists articulated a doctrine similar to the American exculpatory doctrine— confessions or evidence obtained under coercion are inadmissible at trial. Interestingly, some jurists even asserted that judges who rely on a coerced confession in a criminal conviction are to be held liable for wrongful conviction. Most argued that the defendant or his family may bring an action for compensation against the judge individually, and the Caliph and his representatives generally, because the government is deemed vicariously liable for the unlawful behavior of its judges.[32]

But perhaps the most intriguing discourse on the subject in the juristic tradition concerns the rights of God and the rights of people. The rights of God (*huquq Allah*) are rights retained by God in the sense that only God can say how the violation of these rights may be punished and only God has the right to forgive such violations. These rights are subject to the exclusive jurisdiction and dominion of God, and human beings have no choice but to follow the explicit and detailed rules that God set out for handling acts that fall within God's jurisdiction. But all rights not explicitly retained by God are retained by people. And while violations of God's rights are forgiven only by God through adequate acts of repentance, the rights of people may be forgiven only by the people.[33] Thus, according to the juristic tradition, a right to compensation is retained individually by a human being and may be forgiven only by the aggrieved individual. Neither the government nor God has the right to forgive or compromise such a right of compensation if it is designated as part of the rights of human beings. Therefore, the Maliki jurist Ibn al-ʿArabi (d. 543/1148) states:

> The rights of human beings are not forgiven by God unless the human being concerned forgives them first, and the claims for such rights are not dismissed [by God] unless they are dismissed by the person concerned. . . . The rights of a Muslim cannot be abandoned except by the possessor of the right. Even the imam [ruler] does not have the right to demand [or abandon] such rights. This is because the imam is not empowered to act as the agent of a specific set of individuals over their specific rights. Rather, the imam only represents people, generally, for their general and unspecified rights.[34]

In a similar context, the Hanafi jurist al-ʿAyini (d. 855/1451) argues that the usurper of property, even if a government official (al-zalim), will not be forgiven for his sin—even if he repents a thousand times—unless he returns the stolen property.[35] Most of these discourses occur in the context of addressing personal monetary and property rights, but they have not been extended to other civil rights, such as the right to due process or the right to listen, reflect, and study, which may not be violated by the government under any circumstances. This is not because the range of people's rights was narrow—quite the contrary; it is because the range of these rights was too broad. It should be recalled that people retain any rights not explicitly reserved by God. Effectively, since the rights retained by God are quite narrow, the rights accruing to the benefit of people are numerous. The juristic practice has tended to focus on narrow legal claims that may be addressed through the processes of law rather than on broad theoretical categories that were perceived as nonjusticiable before a court. As such, the jurists tended to focus on tangible property rights or rights for compensation instead of moral claims. So, for instance, if one person burns another person's books, the aggrieved party may seek compensation for the destruction of his or her property but cannot bring an action for injunctive relief preventing the burning of the books in the first place. Despite this limitation, the juristic tradition did, in fact, develop a notion of individual claims that are immune from governmental or social limitation or alienation.

One other important aspect needs to be explored in this context. Muslim jurists asserted the rather surprising position that if the rights of God and of people (mixed rights) overlap, in most cases, the rights of people should prevail. The justification for this was that humans need their rights and need to vindicate those rights on earth. God, by contrast, asserts God's rights only for the benefit of human beings, and, in all cases, God can vindicate God's rights in the Hereafter if need be. But Muslim jurists did not imagine a set of unwavering and generalizable rights for each individual at all times. Rather, they thought of individual rights as arising from a legal cause brought about by the suffering of a legal wrong. A person does not possess a right until he or she has been wronged and obtains a claim for retribution or compensation as a result. To shift paradigms would require a transformation of traditional conceptions of rights, so that rights become the property of individual holders, regardless of whether there is a legal cause of action. The set of rights recognized as immutable are those that are necessary to achieve a just society while promoting the element of mercy. In my view, these must be the rights that guarantee the physical safety and moral dignity of every human being. It is quite possible that the relevant individual rights are the five values mentioned earlier, but this issue needs to be reanalyzed in light of the current diversity of human existence. The fact that the rights of people take priority over the rights of God, on this earth, necessarily means that a claimed right of God may not be used to violate the rights of human beings. God is capable of vindicating whichever rights God wishes to vindicate in the Hereafter. On this earth, we concern ourselves only with discovering and establishing the rights that are needed to enable human beings to achieve a just life while, to the extent possible, honoring the asserted rights of God.[36] In this context, the commitment to human rights does not signify a lack of commitment to God or a lack of willingness to obey God, but is instead a necessary part of celebrating human diversity, honoring God's vicegerents, achieving mercy, and pursuing the ultimate goal of justice.

Interestingly, it is not the premodern juristic tradition that poses the greatest barrier to the development of individual rights in Islam. Rather, in my view, the most serious obstacle comes from modern Muslims themselves.[37] Especially in the second half of the last century, a considerable number of Muslims have made the unfounded assumption that Islamic law is concerned primarily with duties, not rights, and that the Islamic conception of rights is collectivist, not individualist. Both assumptions, however, are based only on cultural suppositions about the non-Western "other." It is as if these interpreters fixed on a Judeo-Christian or perhaps Western conception of rights and assumed that Islam must be different.

In reality, claims about both individual and collective rights are largely anachronistic. Premodern Muslim jurists did not assert a collectivist vision of rights or an individualist vision. They did speak of *al-ḥaqq al-ʿamm* (public rights) and often asserted that public rights ought to be given precedence over private entitlements. But this amounted to no more than an assertion that the many should not be made to suffer for the entitlements of the few. For example, as a legal maxim, this was utilized to justify the notion of public tak-

ings or the right to public easements over private property. This
principle was also utilized in prohibiting unqualified doctors from
practicing medicine.[38] But as noted earlier, Muslim jurists did not,
for instance, justify the killing or torture of individuals in order to
promote the welfare of the state or the public interest.

Perhaps the widespread assertion of a primacy of collectivist
and duty-based perspectives in Islam points to the reactive nature
of much contemporary discourse on Islamic law. But the notion
of individual rights is actually easier to justify in Islam than a collectivist orientation. God created human beings as individuals,
and their liability in the Hereafter is individually determined as
well. To commit oneself to safeguarding and protecting the well-
being of individuals is to take God's creation seriously. Each individual embodies a virtual universe of divine miracles. Why should
a Muslim commit him- or herself to the rights and well-being of a
fellow human being? The answer is that God already made such a
commitment when God invested so much of the God-self in each
and every person. This is why the Qur'an asserts that whoever
kills a fellow human being unjustly has in effect murdered all of
humanity; it is as if the killer has murdered the divine sanctity and
defiled the very meaning of divinity (5:32).

Moreover, the Qur'an does not differentiate between the sanctity of a Muslim and that of a non-Muslim.[39] As the Qur'an repeatedly asserts, no human being can limit the divine mercy in any
way or even regulate who is entitled to it (2:105, 3:74, 35:2, 38:9,
39:38, 40:7, 43:32). I take this to mean that non-Muslims as well as
Muslims can be the recipients and givers of divine mercy. The
measure of moral virtue on this earth is a person's proximity to divinity through justice, and not a religious label. The measure in
the Hereafter is a different matter, but that matter is God's exclusive jurisdiction. God will most certainly vindicate God's rights in

the Hereafter in the fashion that God deems most fitting. But our primary moral responsibility on earth is the vindication of the rights of human beings. A commitment in favor of human rights is a commitment in favor of God's creation and, ultimately, a commitment in favor of God.

SHARIʿAH AND THE DEMOCRATIC STATE

A case for democracy presented from within Islam must accept the idea of God's sovereignty; it cannot substitute popular sovereignty for divine sovereignty but must instead show how popular sovereignty—with its idea that citizens have rights and a correlative responsibility to pursue justice with mercy—expresses God's authority, properly understood. Similarly, it cannot reject the idea that God's law is given prior to human action but must show how democratic lawmaking respects that priority.

I have reserved the issue of Shariʿah and the state for the end of my essay because it was necessary to first lay the foundation for addressing it. As part of this foundation, it is important to appreciate the centrality of Shariʿah to Muslim life. Shariʿah is God's Way; it is represented by a set of normative principles, methodologies for the production of legal injunctions, and a set of positive legal rules. As is well known, Shariʿah encompasses a variety of schools of thought and approaches, all of which are equally valid and equally orthodox.[40] Nevertheless, Shariʿah as a whole, with all its schools and variant points of view, remains the Way and law of God.[41]

Shariʿah, for the most part, is not explicitly dictated by God. Rather, Shariʿah relies on the interpretive act of a human agent for its production and execution. Paradoxically, however, Shariʿah is the core value that society must serve. The paradox here is exemplified in the tension between the obligation to live by God's law and the fact that this law is manifested only through subjective interpretive determinations. Even if there is a unified realization that a particular positive command does express the divine law, there is still a vast array of possible subjective executions and applications. This dilemma was resolved to some extent in Islamic discourses by distinguishing between Shariʿah and *fiqh*. Shariʿah, it was argued, is the divine ideal, standing as if suspended in midair, unaffected and uncorrupted by life's vagaries. Fiqh is the human attempt to understand and apply that ideal. Therefore, Shariʿah is immutable, immaculate, and flawless; fiqh is not.[42]

As part of the doctrinal foundations for this discourse, Sunni jurists focused on the tradition attributed to the Prophet, stating: "Every *mujtahid* [jurist who strives to find the correct answer] is correct," or "Every mujtahid will be [justly] rewarded."[43] This implied that there could be more than a single correct answer to the same question. For Sunni jurists, this raised the issue of the purpose of or motivation behind the search for the divine will. What is the divine purpose of setting out indicators to the divine law and then requiring that human beings engage in a search? If the divine wants human beings to reach *the* correct understanding, then how could every interpreter or jurist be correct? Put differently, is there a correct legal response to all legal problems, and are Muslims charged with the legal obligation of finding that response?

The overwhelming majority of Sunni jurists agreed that good faith diligence in searching for the divine will is sufficient to protect a researcher from liability before God.[44] Beyond this, the jurists were divided into two main camps. The first school, known as the *mukhatti'ah*, argued that every legal problem ultimately has a correct answer; however, only God knows the correct response, and the truth will not be revealed until the Final Day. Human beings for the most part cannot conclusively know whether they have found the correct response. In this sense, every mujtahid is correct in trying to find the answer; however, one reader might reach the truth while the rest might mistake it. God, on the Final Day, will inform all readers of who was right and who was wrong. Correctness here means that the mujtahid is to be commended for making the effort, but it does not mean that all responses are equally valid.[45]

The second school, known as the *musawwibah,* argued that there is no specific and correct answer (*hukm muʿayyan*) that God wants human beings to discover; after all, if there were a correct answer, God would have made the evidence indicating a divine rule conclusive and clear.[46] God cannot charge human beings with the duty to find the correct answer when there is no objective means of discovering the correctness of a textual or legal problem. If there were an objective truth to everything, God would have made such a truth ascertainable in this life. Legal truth, or correctness, in most circumstances depends on belief and evidence, and the validity of a legal rule or act is often contingent on the rules of recognition that provide for its existence. Human beings are not charged with the obligation of finding some abstract or inaccessible, legally correct result. Rather, they are charged with the duty to diligently investigate a problem and then follow the results of their own *ijtihad* (judgment or opinion). Al-Juwayni elaborates on this point by noting that "[t]he most a mujtahid would claim is a preponderance of belief [*ghalabat al-zann*] and the balancing of the evidence. However, certainty was never claimed by any of them [the early jurists]. . . . If we were charged with finding [the truth,] we would not have been forgiven for failing to find it."[47] According to al-Juwayni, what God wants or intends is for human beings to search—to live a life fully and thoroughly engaged with the divine. Al-Juwayni explains: it is as if God has said to human beings, "My command to My servants is in accordance with the preponderance of their beliefs. So whoever preponderantly believes that they are obligated to do something, acting upon it becomes My command."[48] God's command to human beings is to diligently search, and God's law is suspended until a human being forms a preponderance of belief about the law. At the point that a preponderance of belief is formed, God's law comes in accordance with the preponderance of belief formed by that particular individual. In sum, if a person honestly and sincerely believes that such and such is the law of God, then for that person it is in fact God's law.[49]

The position of the second school in particular raises difficult questions about the application of the Shari'ah in society.[50] This position implies that God's law is to search for God's law; otherwise the legal charge (*taklif*) is entirely dependent on the subjectivity and sincerity of belief. Under the first school of thought, whatever law the state applies is only potentially the law of God, and we will not find out until the Final Day. Under the second school of thought, any law applied by the state is not the law of God unless the person to which it applies believes it to be God's will and command. The first school suspends knowledge until we are done living, and the second school hinges knowledge to the validity of the process and ultimate sincerity of belief.

Building upon this intellectual heritage, I would suggest that Shari'ah ought to stand in an Islamic polity as a symbolic construct for the divine perfection that is unreachable by human effort. As Ibn Qayyim stated, this is the epitome of justice, goodness, and beauty as conceived and retained by God. Its perfection is preserved, so to speak, in the Mind of God, but anything that is channeled through human agency is necessarily marred by human imperfection. Put differently, Shariʿah as conceived by God is flawless, but as understood by human beings is imperfect and contingent. Jurists ought to continue to explore the ideal of Shariʿah and to expound their imperfect attempts at understanding God's perfection. As long as the argument constructed is normative, it is unfulfilled potential to reach the divine will. Significantly, any law applied is necessarily an unrealized potentiality. Shariʿah is not simply a collection of *ahkam* (a set of positive rules) but also a set of principles, a methodology, and a discursive process that searches for divine ideals. As such, Shariʿah is a work in progress that is never complete.

To put it more concretely: if a legal opinion is adopted and enforced by the state, it cannot be said to be God's law. By passing through the determinative and enforcement processes of the state, the legal opinion is no longer simply a potential—it has become an actual law, applied and enforced. But what has been applied and enforced is not God's law; it is the state's law. Effectively, a religious state law is a contradiction in terms. Either the law belongs to the state or it belongs to God, and as long as the law relies on the subjective agency of the state for its articulation and enforcement, any law enforced by the state is necessarily not God's law. Otherwise, we must be willing to admit that the failure of the law of the state is in fact the failure of God's law and ultimately of God Himself. In Islamic theology, this possibility cannot be entertained.[51]

Of course, the most formidable challenge to this position is the argument that God and His Prophet have set out clear legal injunctions that cannot be ignored. Arguably, God provided unambiguous laws precisely because God wished to limit the role of

human agency and foreclose the possibility of innovations. But—
to return one last time to a point I have emphasized throughout—
regardless of how clear and precise the statements of the Qur'an
and Sunna are, the meaning derived from these sources is negotiated through human agency. For example, the Qur'an states: "As
to the thief, male or female, cut off [*faqta'u*] their hands as a recompense for that which they committed, a punishment from
God, and God is all-powerful and all-wise" (5:38). Although the
legal import of the verse seems clear, it requires at a minimum
that human agents struggle with the meaning of "thief," "cut off,"
"hands," and "recompense." The Qur'an uses the expression
iqta'u, from the root word *qata'a*, which could mean to sever or
cut off but could also mean to deal firmly, to bring to an end, to restrain, or to distance oneself.[52] Whatever the meaning derived
from the text, can the human interpreter claim with certainty that
the determination reached is identical to God's? And even when
the issue of meaning is resolved, can the law be enforced in such
a fashion that one can claim that the result belongs to God? Although God's knowledge and justice are perfect, it is impossible
for human beings to determine or enforce the law in such a fashion that the possibility of a wrongful result is entirely excluded.
This does not mean that the exploration of God's law is pointless;
it means only that the interpretations of jurists are potential ful-
fillments of the divine will, but the laws as codified and implemented by the state cannot be considered the actual fulfillment of
these potentialities.

Institutionally, it is consistent with the Islamic experience that
the ulema can and do act as the interpreters of the divine word,
the custodians of the moral conscience of the community, and the
curators who point the nation toward the ideal that is God.[53] But
the law of the state, regardless of its origins or basis, belongs to

the state. Under this conception, no religious laws can or may be enforced by the state. All laws articulated and applied in a state are thoroughly human and should be treated as such. These laws are a part of Shari‘ah law only to the extent that any set of human legal opinions can be said to be a part of Shari‘ah. A code, even if inspired by Shari‘ah, is not Shari‘ah. Put differently, creation, with all its textual and nontextual richness, can and should produce foundational rights and organizational laws that honor and promote these rights. But these rights and laws do not mirror the perfection of divine creation.

According to this paradigm, democracy is an appropriate system for Islam because it both expresses the special worth of human beings—the status of vicegerency—and at the same time deprives the state of any pretense of divinity by locating ultimate authority in the hands of the people rather than the ulema. Moral educators have a serious role to play because they must be vigilant in urging society to approximate God. But not even the will of the majority—no matter how well educated morally—can embody the full majesty of God. And in the worst case—if the majority is not persuaded by the ulema, if the majority insists on turning away from God but still respects the fundamental rights of individuals, including the right to ponder creation and call to the way of God—those individuals who constituted the majority will still have to answer, in the Hereafter, to God.

NOTES

I am grateful to my wife, Grace, for her invaluable feedback and assistance. I thank Anver Emon and Mairaj Syed, my research assistants, for their diligent work on this chapter, and I also thank my assistant, Naheed Fakoor, for competently managing everything related to the timely production of my work. I am especially grateful to Joshua Cohen and Fred

Appel, who believed in the importance of this project and who gener-
ously dedicated numerous hours of their time in order to ensure the suc-
cessful completion of this book. My work is much richer because of their
valuable insights. I am indebted to the staff at *Boston Review,* which was
the first to suggest and promote this project, and I also thank the Boston
NPR radio affiliate WBUR and its radio program, "On Point," *www.
onpointradio.org,* which gave this project moral support and publicity.

1. Abu al-Hasan al-Mawardi, *al-Ahkam al-Sultaniyya* (Beirut: Dar al-
Kutub al-'Ilmiyya, 1985), 19–21; al-Qadi Abu Ya'la al-Farra', *al-Ahkam al-
Sultaniyya* (Beirut: Dar al-Kutub al-'Ilmiyya, 1983), 28; Yusuf Ibish, *Nusus
al-Fikr al-Siyasi al-Islami: al-Imama 'ind al-Sunna* (Beirut: Dar al-Tali'ah,
1966), 55; Nizam Barakat, *Muqaddima fi al-Fikr al-Siyasi al-Islami*
(Riyadh: Jami'at al-Malik Su'ud, 1985), 119.

2. Muhammad b. 'Ali al-Shawkani, *Nayl al-Awtar Sharh Muntaqa al-
Akhbar* (Cairo: Dar al-Hadith, n.d.), 7:166; Shihab al-Din Ibn Hajar al-
'Asqalani, *Fath al-Bari bi Sharh Sahih al-Bukhari* (Beirut: Dar al-Fikr,
1993), 14:303.

3. Ironically, Shi'i and Sunni fundamentalist groups detest the
Khawarij and consider them heretics, but this is not because these modern groups disagree with the Khawarij's political slogans but because the
Khawarij murdered 'Ali, the cousin of the Prophet. Epistemologically,
however, the similiarities between modern-day fundamentalist groups
and the premodern Khawarij are numerous and undeniable.

4. According to the Qur'an, God, at the moment of creation, as a symbol of the honor due to human beings, commanded the angels, who are
incapable of sin, to prostrate themselves before Adam. The angels
protested that God was commanding them to honor a being that is capable of sin and that is bound to commit evil and cause mischief. God af-
firmed that human beings are capable of causing much mischief but
explained that the miracle of the intellect, in and of itself, deserves to be
honored, and that furthermore, God had made human beings the
vicegerents of divinity. Not having any choice but to obey, the angels
prostrated themselves before Adam, but Satan, who was from the jinn
and not an angel, defied God and refused to prostrate himself. Satan's attitude can be described as dismissive of the intellect, bigoted, and even
ethnocentric. Satan argued that he was created of fire and Adam was created of clay, and, according to Satan, everyone knows that fire is superior
to clay. Therefore, it was inconceivable that he would have to prostrate

himself before Adam. As a result of this anti-intellect position and as a consequence of his disobedience, Satan was damned through eternity. On this, see Fazlur Rahman, *Major Themes of the Qur'an* (Minneapolis: Bibliotheca Islamica, 1994), 17–36.

5. One of the most important treatises, but also one of the most ne-glected, was written by Hasan Isma'il al-Hudaybi, a former chairman of the Muslim Brotherhood in Egypt, in which he effectively refuted the no-tion that divine hakimiyya means that God is the only legitimate legisla-tor. Al-Hudaybi argued that political sovereignty, as opposed to moral sovereignty, belongs to the citizens of the state. Rather tellingly, the au-thor's arguments, despite their liberal implications, would have been far more persuasive to medieval Muslim jurists than they are to contempo-rary fundamentalist activists. See Hasan Isma'il al-Hudaybi, *Du'ah la Qudah* (Cairo: Dar al-Nashr al-Islamiyya, 1977).

6. 'Abd Ya'la al-Farra', "al-Mu'tamad fi Usul al-Din," in *Nusus al-Fikr,* by Ibish, 196, 199; Abu Hamid al-Ghazali, *Fada'ih al-Batiniyya,* ed. 'Abd al-Rahman Badawi (Cairo: Dar al-Qawmiyya, 1964), 135–37; Abu Hasan al-Mawardi, *Adab al-Dunya wa al-Din,* ed. Mustafa al-Saqqa (Cairo: n.p., 1950), 5.

7. 'Abd Allah b. Muslim b. Qutayba [attributed], *al-Imama wa al-Siyasa,* ed. Zini Taha (Cairo: Mu'assasat al-Halabi, 1967), 21. This book is traditionally known as *Ta'rikh al-Khulafa'*.

8. The Mu'tazilah was a theological school of thought whose adher-ents called themselves *ahl al-'adl wa al-tawhid* (the people of justice and unity). The school traces its origins to the thought of Wasil b. 'Ata' (d. 131/748) in Basra. The Mu'tazilah are often described as rationalists because of their emphasis on rational theology. They also considered jus-tice and enjoining the good and forbidding the evil among the five basic principles of faith. The Mu'tazilah's five principles of faith were (1) *tawhid* (belief in the unity and singularity of God); (2) *'adl* (justice); (3) *al-wa'd wa al-wa'id* (the promise of reward and threat of punish-ment); (4) *al-manzilah bayna al-manzilatayn* (those who commit a major sin are neither believers nor nonbelievers); (5) *al-amr bi al-ma-'ruf wa al-nahy 'an al-munkar* (commanding the good and prohibiting the evil).

9. Citing the precedent of the Prophet in Medina, al-Asam maintained that this included free Muslim women, but not non-Muslims or slaves. Re-portedly, upon migrating to Medina, the Prophet took the *bay'a* from a

number of native women as well as men. Muhammad ʿImara, *al-Islam wa Falsafat al-Hukm* (Beirut: n.p., 1979), 431–32.

10. Ibid., 435.

11. For instance, see al-Mawardi, *al-Ahkam al-Sultaniyya*, 18; Taqi al-Din Ibn Taymiyyah, *al-Siyasah al-Sharʿiyyah* (Beirut: Dar al-Afaq al-Jadidah, 1983), 142.

12. On the prohibition against women driving automobiles, see my *Speaking in God's Name: Islamic Law, Authority, and Women* (Oxford: Oneworld Publications, 2001), 235, 272–73, 278–80.

13. For example, in 1801, after the evacuation of the French in Egypt, ʿUmar Makram, with the assistance of the Egyptian jurists, overthrew the French agent who was left behind. Instead of assuming power directly, however, the jurists offered the government to the Egyptianized Albanian Muhammad ʿAli.

14. Afaf Lutfi al-Sayyid Marsot, "The Ulama of Cairo in the Eighteenth and Nineteenth Century," in *Scholars, Saints, and Sufis*, ed. Nikki Keddi (Berkeley: University of California Press, 1972), 149.

15. Daniel Crecelius, "Egyptian Ulama and Modernization," in *Scholars, Saints, and Sufis*, ed. Nikki Keddi (Berkeley: University of California Press, 1972), 167–209, 168. Of course, in contemporary Islamic practice, there are notable exceptions. Many clerics became prominent opponents of contemporary Muslim regimes and suffered enormously for their troubles.

16. ʿAbd al-Wahhab Khallaf, *ʿIlm Usul al-Fiqh* (Kuwait: Dar al-Qalam, 1981), 59.

17. Jalal al-Din ʿAbd al-Rahman al-Suyuti, *Taʾrikh al-Khulafaʾ*, ed. Ibrahim Abu al-Fadl (Cairo: Dar al-Nahda, 1976), 109.

18. Al-Ghazali, *Fadaʾih*, 186, 191; Muhammad Jalal Sharaf and ʿAli ʿAbd al-Muʿti Muhammad, *al-Fikr al-Siyasi fi al-Islam: Shakhsiyyat wa Madhahib* (Alexandria: Dar al-Jamiʿat al-Misriyya, 1978), 399–403.

19. On the obligation of justice in the Qurʾan, see Rahman, *Major Themes of the Qurʾan*, 42–43; Toshihiko Izutsu, *The Structure of Ethical Terms in the Qurʾan* (Chicago: ABC International Group, 2000), 205–61. On the various Muslim theories of justice, see Majid Khadduri, *The Islamic Conception of Justice* (Baltimore: Johns Hopkins University Press, 1984).

20. An excerpt in Qurʾan 21:107, addressing the Prophet, states: "We have not sent you except as a mercy to human beings." See also Qurʾan

16:89. In fact, the Qur'an describes the whole of the Islamic message as based on mercy and compassion. Islam was sent to teach and establish these virtues among human beings. I believe that as to Muslims, as opposed to Islam, this creates a normative imperative of teaching mercy (27:77, 29:51, 45:20). But to teach mercy is impossible unless one learns it, and such knowledge cannot be limited to the text. This is *ta'aruf* (social intercourse that leads to true and genuine knowledge of the other), which is premised on an ethic of care that opens the door to learning mercy and in turn to teaching it.

21. In Qur'anic terms, *rahma* (mercy) is not limited to *maghfira* (forgiveness).

22. The Qur'an explicitly commands human beings to deal with one another with patience and mercy (90:17) and not to transgress their bounds by presuming to know who deserves God's mercy and who does not (43:32). An Islamic moral theory focused on mercy as a virtue overlaps with the ethic of care developed in Western moral theory.

23. This idea is also exemplified in a tradition attributed to the Prophet asserting that the disagreement and diversity of opinions of the *umma* (Muslim nation) is a source of divine mercy for Muslims. See Isma'il al-Jirahi, *Kashf al-Khafa' wa Muzil al-Ilbas* (Beirut: Mu'assasat al-Risala, 1983), 1:66–68. Whether the Prophet actually made this statement or this statement is part of the received wisdom that guided the diverse and often competing interpretive traditions within Islam is beside the point. The point is that this tradition, Prophetic or not, was used to justify an enormous amount of diversity within the Islamic juristic tradition, and it played an important role in preventing the emergence of a single voice of authority within the Islamic tradition. On this issue, see Khaled Abou El Fadl, *And God Knows the Soldiers: The Authoritative and Authoritarian in Islamic Discourses* (Landham, Md.: University Press of America, 2001), 23–36.

24. Of course, approximating the divine does not mean aspiring to become divine. Approximating the divine means visualizing the beauty and virtue of the divine and striving to internalize as much as possible of this beauty and virtue. I start with the theological assumption that God cannot be comprehended or understood by the human mind. God, however, teaches moral virtues that emanate from the divine nature and that are also reflected in creation. By imagining the possible magnitudes of beauty and its nature, human beings can better relate to the divine. The

more humans are able to relate to the ultimate sense of goodness, justice, mercy, and balance, which embody divinity, the more they can visualize, or imagine, the nature of divinity, and the more they are able to model their own sense of beauty and virtue as approximations of divinity.

25. Abu Hamid Muhammad al-Ghazali, *al-Mustasfa min ʿIlm al-Usul,* ed. Ibrahim Muhammad Ramadan (Beirut: Dar al-Arqam, n.d.), 1:286–87; Fakhr al-Din Muhammad b. ʿUmar b. al-Husayn al-Razi, *al-Mahsul fi ʿIlm al-Usul,* ed. Taha Jabir al-ʿAlwani (Beirut: Muʾassasat al-Risalah, 1997), 5:159–60; Abu Ishaq Ibrahim al-Shatibi, *al-Muwafaqat fi Usul al-Fiqh,* ed. ʿAbd Allah Daraz and Muhammad ʿAbd Allah Daraz (Beirut: Dar al-Kutub al-ʿIlmiyya, n.d.), 2:7–8; Shihab al-Din al-Qarafi, *Sharh Tanqih al-Fusul,* ed. Taha Abd al-Raʾuf Saʿd (Beirut: Dar al-Fikr, 1973), 391; Mohammad Hashim Kamali, *Principles of Islamic Jurisprudence* (Cambridge: Islamic Texts Society, 1991), 271–73.

26. Muhammad ʿUbayd Allah al-Asʿadi, *al-Mujaz fi Usul al-Fiqh* (n.p.: Dar al-Salam, 1990), 247; Badran Abu al-ʿAynayn Badran, *Usul al-Fiqh* (Cairo: Dar al-Maʾrifa, 1965), 430–31; Zakariyya al-Birri, *Usul al-Fiqh al-Islami,* 3d ed. (Cairo: Dar al-Nahdah al-ʿArabiyya, 1974), 144–45; Wahbah al-Zuhayli, *al-Wasit fi Usul al-Fiqh,* 2d ed. (Beirut: Dar al-Fikr, 1969), 498–99; Muhammad Abu Zahra, *Usul al-Fiqh* (Cairo: Dar al-Fikr al-ʿArabi, n.d.), 291–93; Ali Hasab Allah, *Usul al-Tashriʿ al-Islami* (Cairo: Dar al-Maʾrifa, 1964), 260; Zaki al-Din Shaʿban, *Usul al-Fiqh al-Islami* (Cairo: Matbaʾat Dar al-Taʾlif, 1965), 382–84.

27. I would argue that the definition of the protection of religion should be developed to mean protecting the freedom of religious belief; the protection of life should mean that the taking of life must be for a just cause and the result of a just process; the protection of the intellect should mean the right to free thinking, expression, and belief; the protection of honor should mean the protection of the dignity of a human being; and the protection of property should mean the right to compensation for the taking of property.

28. Jalal al-Din ʿAbd al-Rahman al-Suyuti, *al-Ashbah wa Nazaʾir fi Qawaʿid wa Furuʿ al-Shafiʿiyya* (Beirut: Dar al-Kutub al-ʿIlmiyya, 1983), 53; ʿAli Ahmad al-Nadhwi, *al-Qawaʿid al-Fiqhiyya,* 3d ed. (Damascus: Dar al-Qalam, 1994), 400–401; Ahmad b. Muhammad al-Zarqa, *Sharh al-Qawaʿid al-Fiqhiyya,* 4th ed. (Damascus: Dar al-Qalam, 1996), 369–89; al-ʿAsqalani, *Fath al-Bari,* 14:308; Abu Ishaq Burhan al-Din Ibn Muflih, *al-Mubdiʿ fi Sharh al-Muqniʿ* (Beirut: al-Maktab al-Islami, 1980), 9:168.

29. Khaled Abou El Fadl, *Rebellion and Violence in Islamic Law* (Cambridge: Cambridge University Press, 2001), 32, 50–57, 73–77, 340–41.

30. Muslim jurists, however, did not consider the severing of hands or feet—as punishment for theft and banditry—to be mutilation.

31. A considerable number of jurists in Islamic history were persecuted and murdered for holding that a political endorsement (bayʿa) obtaind under duress is invalid. Muslim jurists described the death of these scholars under such circumstances as a death of *musabara* (under perseverance). This had become an important discourse because caliphs were in the habit of either bribing or threatening notables and jurists to obtain their bayʿa. See Abd al-Rahman b. Muhammad Ibn Khaldun, *al-Muqaddima* (Beirut: Dar Ihyaʾ al-Turath, n.d.), 165; Abou El Fadl, *Rebellion and Violence,* 86–87. On the Islamic law of duress and on coerced confessions and coerced votes of allegiance, see Khaled Abou El Fadl, "Law of Duress in Islamic Law and Common Law: A Comparative Study," *Islamic Studies* 30, no. 3 (1991): 305–50.

32. Abu Bakr Ahmad al-Shaybani al-Khassaf, *Kitab Adab al-Qadi,* ed. Farhat Ziyadah (Cairo: American University of Cairo Press, 1978), 364–65; Abu al-Hasan al-Mawardi, *Adab al-Qadi,* ed. Muhyi Hilal al-Sarhan (Baghdad: Matbaʿat al-Irshad, 1971), 1:233; idem, *al-Ahkam al-Sultaniyya,* 58; Abu al-Qasim ʿAli b. Muhammad al-Simnani, *Rawdat al-Qudah wa Tariq al-Najah* (Beirut: Muʾassasat al-Risala, 1984), 1:157–58; *al-Fatawa al-Hindiyya* (Beirut: Dar Ihyaʾ al-Turath al-ʿArabi, 1986), 6:430; ʿUthman b. ʿAli al-Zaylaʿi, *Tabyin al-Haqaʾiq Sharh Kanz al-Daqaʾiq* (Medina: Dar al-Kitab al-Islamiyya, n.d.), 3:240.

33. In juristic sources, these are referred to as *huquq al-ʿibad,* or *huquq al-nas,* or *huquq al-adamiyyin.*

34. Abu Bakr Muhammad b. al-ʿArabi, *Ahkam al-Qurʾan,* ed. ʿAli Muhammad al-Bajawi (Beirut: Dar al-Maʿrifah, n.d.), 2:603.

35. Abu Muhammad Mahmud b. Ahmad al-ʿAyini, *al-Binayah fi Sharh al-Hidayah* (Beirut: Dar al-Fikr, 1990), 6:482.

36. This idea is reflected in a well-known tradition attributed to the Prophet: that whenever God commands humans to do something, then they should do of it as much as they can. This tradition represents a further recognition of the contingent and aspirational nature of human ability and also that while humans may strive for perfection, God is perfection itself.

37. Of course, this is a controversial claim. Most Muslim modernists and reformers have assumed that the Islamic juristic tradition stands as a

serious obstacle to efforts in seeking to develop commitments in favor of democracy and human rights. Even the fanatically conservative Wahhabi movement considers most of the juristic tradition in Islam if not an aberration from the one and only true Islam then at least unnecessary baggage. Quite to the contrary, however, I think that if the juristic tradition is understood in its proper historical context, and if it is treated analytically and critically, it could become a considerable force for principled reform and development. Furthermore, I believe that ignoring or dismissing this impressive interpretive tradition as irrelevant or disposable will serve not to liberate and empower Muslim reformers but to deny them legitimacy and to impoverish them intellectually.

38. Salim Rustum Bazz, *Sharh al-Majalla* (Beirut: Dar Ihya' al-Turath al-'Arabi, 1986), 31, 43–44. Muslim jurists also asserted that specific rights and duties should be given priority over general rights and duties. This legal principle was applied primarily to laws of agency and trust. Although the principle could be expanded and developed to support individual rights in the modern age, historically it was given a far more technical and legalistic connotation.

39. Some premodern jurists did differentiate between Muslims and non-Muslims, especially in matters pertaining to criminal liability and compensation for torts.

40. The four surviving Sunni schools of law and legal thought are the Hanafi, Maliki, Shafi'i, and Hanbali. There are many schools of jurisprudence, such as the Jariri, Awza'i, Zahiri, and Thawri, that have become extinct in the sense that they no longer command a large number of adherents, but the texts of these schools remain extant in many cases.

41. Even the puritanical Wahhabis, who considerably narrow the range and scope of subjects and issues on which Muslims may legitimately disagree, have not been able to deny the validity of this doctrine. The Wahhabis, and other Muslim extremists and literalists, could not deny the legitimacy of the various competing schools of thought in Islam. Rather, their tactic has been to claim the existence of agreement and consensus among the different schools of thought on certain points of law, when in fact agreement does not exist. The Wahhabis also claim that disagreement is acceptable only as to the branches (*furu'*) of religion, but not on the basics and fundamentals (*usul*). However, they proceed to widen the range and scope of the so-called fundamentals of religion to the point that disagreement becomes permissible only on the most marginal issues.

42. I am simplifying this sophisticated doctrine to make a point. Muslim jurists engaged in lengthy attempts to differentiate between the two concepts of Shari'ah and fiqh. See Subhi Mahmasani, *Fasafat al-Tashri' fi al-Islam,* 3d ed. (Beirut: Dar al-'Ilm li al-Malayin, 1961), 21-24, 199-200; Abu Zahra, *Usul al-Fiqh,* 291; Mustafa Zayd, *al-Maslaha fi Tashri' al-Islam wa Najm al-Din al-Tufi,* 2d ed. (Cairo: Dar al-Fikr al-'Arabi, 1964), 22; Yusuf Hamid al-'Alim, *al-Maqasid al-'Ammah li al-Shari'ah al-Islamiyya* (Herndon, Va.: International Institute of Islamic Thought, 1991), 80; Muhammad b. 'Ali al-Shawkani, *Talab al-'Ilm wa Tabaqat al-Muta'allimin: Adab al-Talab wa Muntaha al-'Arab* (n.p.: Dar al-Arqam, 1981), 145-51.

43. In this context, Sunni jurists also debated a report attributed to the Prophet in which he says, "Whoever performs ijtihad and is correct will be rewarded twice, and whoever is wrong will be rewarded once." See Abu al-Husayn Muhammad al-Basri, *al-Mu'tamad fi Usul al-Fiqh* (Beirut: Dar al-Kutub al-'Ilmiyya, 1983), 2:370-72; al-Ghazali, *al-Mustasfa,* 2:363-67; Abu al-Ma'ali 'Abd al-Malik al-Juwayni, *Kitab al-Ijtihad min Kitab al-Talkhis* (Damascus: Dar al-Qalam, 1987), 26-32; al-Qarafi, *Sharh,* 438-41; al-Razi, *al-Mahsul,* 6:29-36; Jalal al-Din 'Abd al-Rahman al-Suyuti, *Ikthilaf al-Madhahib,* ed. 'Abd al-Qayyum Muhammad al-Bastawi (Cairo: Dar al-I'tisam, A.H. 1404), 38; Muhammad b. Idris al-Shafi'i, *al-Risalah,* ed. Ahmad Muhammad Shakir (n.p.: Dar al-Fikr, n.d.), 494; Abu Ishaq Yusuf al-Fayruzabadi al-Shirazi, *al-Tabsira fi Usul al-Fiqh* (Damascus: Dar al-Fikr, 1980), 499.

44. This juristic position is to be distinguished from the early theological school of the Murji'a (Murji'ites) of the school of the suspension of judgment. The school of the Murji'a developed in reaction to the fanaticism of the Khawarij, who believed that the commission of a major sin renders a Muslim a nonbeliever. The Murji'a believed that major sins are offset by faith and argued that punishment in the Hereafter is not everlasting. They also refused to take a position on political disputes, arguing that judgment over any political dispute ought to be suspended until the Final Day. Most of the jurists I describe here did not adhere to Murji'i theology.

45. Literalist schools of thought, including the modern-day Wahhabis, agree with this perspective, but they insist that when the Prophet declared that every mujtahid will be rewarded, the Prophet meant this to apply only to an exceedingly narrow range of issues, on which the text is

vague or ambiguous. The literalists and extremist schools, in general, claim that the divine text is clear and unambiguous as to the vast majority of matters, and therefore, on most issues, there can be only one legitimate position or answer. Nonetheless, these literalists, and especially the Wahhabis, lack a methodology for systematically distinguishing between text that is clear, precise, and unambiguous and text that is not. In the final analysis, a text is considered unambiguous and clear because the Wahhabis say it is so.

46. For discussions of the two schools, see ʿAla' al-Din b. Ahmai al-Bukhari, *Kashf al-Asrar ʿan Usul Fakhr al-Islam,* ed. Muhammad al-Muʾtasin bi Allah (Beirut: Dar al-Kitab al-Arabi, 1997), 4:18; Abu Hamid Muhammad al-Ghazali, *al-Mankhul min Taʿliqat al-Usul* (Damascus: Dar al-Fikr, 1980), 455; idem, *al-Mustasfa,* 2:550–51; al-Razi, *al-Mahsul,* 2:500–508; al-Qarafi, *Sharh,* 438; al-Zuhayli, *al-Wasit,* 638–55; Hasab Allah, *Usul al-Tashrīʿ,* 82–83; Badran, *Usul al-Fiqh,* 474.

47. Al-Juwayni, *Kitab al-Ijtihad,* 50–51.

48. Ibid., 61.

49. Sayf al-Din Abu al-Hasan ʿAli b. Abi ʿAli b.Muhammad al-Amidi, *al-Ihkam fi Usul al-Ahkam,* ed. ʿAbd al-Razzaq ʿAfifi, 2d ed. (Beirut: al-Maktab al-Islami, A.H. 1402), 4:183; Jamal al-Din Abi Muhammad ʿAbd al-Rahim b. al-Hasan al-Asnawi, *al-Tamhid fi Takhrij al-Furuʿ ʿala al-Usul,* 3d ed. (Beirut: Muʾassasat al-Risalah, 1984), 531–34; Muhammad b. al-Hasan al-Badakhshi, *Sharh al-Badakhshi Manahij al-ʿUqul maʿa Sharh al-Asnawi Nihayat al-Sul* (Beirut: Dar al-Kutub al-ʿIlmiyya, 1984), 3:275–81; Abu H amid al-Ghazali, *al-Mustasfa,* 2:375–78; al-Juwayni, *Kitab al-Ijtihad,* 41; Abu al-Thana' Mahmud b. Zayd al-Lamishi, *Kitab fi Usul al-Fiqh,* ed. ʿAbd al-Majid Turki (Beirut: Dar al-Gharb al-Islami, 1995), 202–3; al-Qarafi, *Sharh,* 440; al-Din al-Razi, *al-Mahsul,* 6:34–35, 6:43–50.

50. I deal much more extensively with these two schools of thought and their potential impact on modern Islam in my book *Speaking in God's Name.*

51. I would go further and argue that the idea of state-implemented Shariʿah law could potentially establish and promote an idolatrous paradigm. Shariʿah is synonymous with divine perfection and immutability. The modern state, with all its human imperfections, cannot claim to represent or embody the divine perfection without falling into a paradigm that is idolatrous because, in effect, the state is claiming that it can partake in, share in, or even represent the divine perfection. This is theologically

problematic, to say the least. In this regard, contemporary Islamic discourses suffer from a certain measure of hypocrisy. Often, Muslims confront a public relations crisis when the enforced, so-called state Shari'ah laws result in social hardship, suffering, or misery. In response to this crisis, Muslims often have claimed that there was a failure in the circumstances of implementation or that the divine law was not properly implemented. This indulgence in embarrassing apologetics could be avoided if Muslims would abandon the incoherent idea of Shari'ah state law.

52. Al-'Allamah Ibn Manzur, *Lisan al-'Arab* (Riyadh: Dar al-Thabat, 1997), 11:220–28. Ahmed Ali argues in that the word used in the Qur'an does not mean to amputate a limb but rather, to "stop their hands from stealing by adopting deterrent means" (Ahmed Ali, *Al-Qur'an* [Princeton: Princeton University Press], 113). In classical jurisprudence, jurists placed conditions that were practically impossible to fulfill before a limb could be amputated.

53. To regain their persuasive authority as curators of morality and interpreters and advocates of Shari'ah, and to play an effective mediating role in civil society, the ulema must first regain their institutional and moral independence from the state. As long as the ulema are controlled and directed by the state, their credibility and legitimacy as advocates and agents on behalf of God and Shari'ah will remain seriously suspect.

Responses

CHANGE FROM WITHIN

Nader A. Hashemi

◈ One of the most prescient insights about Islam and democracy that have informed my politics over the years is an observation by the late Eqbal Ahmad, a dissident Pakistani Muslim intellectual.[1] In response to the question, What strategies should Arab and Muslim intellectuals pursue to democratize their societies? he offered the following words of wisdom:

> One must make an effort to understand the past, understand it with compassion, sympathy, and criticism. The reason I am stressing that is that many of us, Arab and Muslim intellectuals, know more about the West, more about modern history, more about the ideas of the Enlightenment than we do about our own [history and culture]. No significant change occurs unless the new form is congruent with the old. It is only when a transplant is congenial to a soil that it works. Therefore, it is very important to know the transplant as well as the native soil.
>
> There is a great deal in our civilization which has been old, very creative, very humane in many areas and also with many weaknesses, with many problems. [It is necessary] for us to understand our own first and then develop change in an

organic relationship to the inherited civilization. We have to visualize change in that way, otherwise it won't work.[2]

I am reminded of these remarks after reading Khaled Abou El Fadl's thoughtful meditation on Islam and the challenge of democracy. Abou El Fadl has made a significant and unique contribution to advancing a democratic theory for Muslim societies by virtue of his command of both the core requirements of modern liberal-democracy and—this is the important part—his solid grasp of Islamic political and theological thought. Very few people within the Muslim world possess a firm grounding in both disciplines—Eqbal Ahmad was one of them—which is one reason liberal democracy remains a contested concept.

Regrettably, democratic voices in the Muslim world have read their own secularity into their host communities, which remain largely religious. On the other side of the equation, Islamically inspired activists who enjoy grassroots support are alienated from the values of democracy and liberalism because they view these as foreign imports tied to a colonial and imperial agenda that lacks cultural authenticity. The result is a dialogue between two deaf segments of Muslim society that desperately need to communicate. Ahmad realized that bridging this chasm was a way of emphasizing that "no significant change occurs unless the new form is congruent with the old. It is only when a transplant is congenial to a soil that it works." We need to "develop change in an organic relationship to the inherited civilization . . . otherwise it won't work." Had Ahmad been alive today, he would have shared my enthusiasm for Abou El Fadl's essay, primarily because it seeks to indigenize democracy and human rights within an Islamic framework.[3]

The second contribution Abou El Fadl has made is refuting a

widely held thesis that Islam is incompatible with democracy. After September 11, 2001, this idea has, understandably, gained new currency. According to Bernard Lewis, the culture of Islam and democracy are fundamentally incongruent and the choice facing Muslims in the twenty-first century is between modernization and fanaticism. "The future of the Middle East will depend on which of them prevails," he recently told an audience at Princeton University.[4] Similarly, Leonard Binder refers to a "cluster of absences" within Islam that accounts for its liberal-democratic deficit: the absence of a concept of liberty, the absence of a middle class, and the absence of autonomous corporate institutions.[5] Although it is tempting to invoke these arguments in today's post–September 11 world, the "Islamic exceptionalist thesis" does not stand up to critical scrutiny.

Like other religious traditions whose origins lie in the premodern era and are scripturally based, Islam is neither more nor less compatible with modern democracy than Christianity or Judaism. Not too long ago it was similarly argued that Catholicism was an obstacle to democracy and that only countries with a Protestant majority respected popular sovereignty. Religious traditions are a highly complex body of ideas, assumptions, and doctrines that when interpreted in a modern context, many centuries or millennia later, contain sufficient ambiguity and elasticity to be read in a variety of ways. This is not to suggest that religious doctrine should be completely ignored when discussing democracy in the Muslim world. At best, it is one factor among many that affect the prospects for political development. Abou El Fadl's point is that Islamic tradition and Muslim political thought are not fossilized, and they are capable of being read and interpreted in myriad distinct ways—including as supporting democracy and liberalism. The current struggle for democracy in Iran is ample proof of this.

While student demonstrators have garnered much deserved international media attention for their opposition to theocratic authoritarianism, a less well known yet equally significant transformation of Iran's religious heritage is under way. Led by dissident clerics, it has had a significant impact on the process of democratization. The liberal and democratic Islamic exegeses of theologians such as Mohsen Kadivar, Mojtahed Shabestari, and Hassan Yousefi Eshkavari have won them a broad following among all layers of society, particularly among the burgeoning youth population. Unable to respond to these ideas in the court of public opinion, the ruling clerical establishment has resorted to censorship, imprisonment, and outright intimidation. In a sermon at Tehran University, for example, the chief conservative ideologue, Mohammad Taqi Mesbah-Yazdi, summed up this new call to arms: "If someone tells you he has a new interpretation of Islam, sock him in the mouth."[6]

The broader lesson that emerges from Abou El Fadl's essay is that the popular question—Is Islam compatible with democracy?—is fundamentally misleading. The real focus should be not on what Islam is but rather on what Muslims want.[7] If Muslims genuinely seek to construct a democratic society in which international standards of human rights are both respected and protected, then it is up to them to invoke the necessary arguments, make the required sacrifices, and engage in an interpretation of their religious tradition that can turn this vision into reality. In this debate, Western societies have very little say on what is fundamentally an internal Muslim struggle. Any intervention will probably make the situation worse. The best thing the West can do is to observe its own ideals when dealing with the Muslim world and to let the struggle for Islamic democracy run its evolutionary course.

POSTSCRIPT ON IRAQ, U.S. FOREIGN POLICY, AND DEMOCRATIZATION

As a general rule, the less the external intervention in the Muslim world the better the prospects for democracy. It cannot be overemphasized that the most powerful organizing theme in the Muslim world is colonialism. In particular, there is a widely held view among Muslims that the chief reason that Islamic civilization has declined and cannot be rejuvenated is past and present victimization by external powers. The ongoing dispossession of the Palestinians by an Israeli state closely tied to the West reinforces this belief. As a result, political concepts and modern ideas such as democracy and human rights have to pass the test of cultural authenticity, especially when they are introduced as a consequence of American military intervention. "The West wants to distract you with shiny slogans like freedom, democracy, culture and civil society," Kadhem al-Ebadi al-Nasseri, a Muslim cleric, told his congregation in Baghdad after the fall of the Baathists. "Infidel corruption has entered our society through these concepts."[8]

Exceptions to this noninterventist rule do exist, especially in the case of genocidal regimes whose totalitarian stranglehold on their population prevents an indigenous movement for political change from emerging. Saddam Hussein's Iraq was one such regime. In the aftermath of his downfall, the challenge that lies ahead is whether the United States is willing to sufficiently disengage and establish a legitimate framework for democratization that gives Iraqis a real voice in the governing of their affairs. Given the legacy of U.S. intervention in the Middle East and recent comments by Deputy Defense Secretary Paul Wolfowitz on Turkish democracy and the role of the military, skepticism is entirely warranted.[9]

NOTES

1. See Carollee Bengelsdorf and Margaret Cerullo, eds., *The Collected Writings of Eqbal Ahmad* (New York: Columbia University Press, forthcoming); Eqbal Ahmad, *Confronting Empire: Interviews with David Barsamian* (Boston: South End Press, 2000); http://bitsonline.net/eqbal/.

2. Unpublished interview with Emran Qureshi, 21 December 1994.

3. Along the same lines, Abdullahi An-Na'im observed that to "seek secular answers [to the Muslim condition] is simply to abandon the field to the fundamentalists, who will succeed in carrying the vast majority of the population with them by citing religious authority for their policies and theories. Intelligent and enlightened Muslims are therefore best advised to remain within the religious framework and endeavor to achieve the reforms that would make Islam a viable modern ideology" (*Toward An Islamic Reformation: Civil Liberties, Human Rights, and International Law* [Syracuse: Syracuse University Press, 1990], xii).

4. Catherine Stevenson, "Lewis Tells Audience of Difficult Choices Facing Islamic World," *Daily Princetonian,* 11 November 2002.

5. Cited by Gudrun Kramer, "Islamist Notions of Democracy," in *Political Islam: Essays from Middle East Report,* ed. Joel Beinin and Joe Stork (Berkeley and Los Angeles: University of California Press, 1997), 71.

6. Reuters, 20 September 1999.

7. I borrow this insight from Graham Fuller, "The Future of Political Islam," *Foreign Affairs* (March–April 2002). Abou El Fadl implicitly acknowledges this point when he writes: "To be sure, these doctrinal potentialities may remain unrealized: without willpower, inspired vision, and moral commitment there can be no democracy in Islam."

8. Susan Sachs, "Shiite Clerics' Ambitions Collide in an Iraqi Slum," *New York Times,* 25 May 2003.

9. After the Iraq war, Paul Wolfowitz appeared on CNN Turk, where he criticized Turkey for not supporting the U.S. war effort. "[L]et's have a Turkey that steps up and says, 'We made a mistake,'" he confidently asserted. He then went on to lament that the Turkish military did not display a "strong leadership role" in determining Turkish foreign policy (U.S. State Department, "Wolfowitz Criticizes Turkey for Not Backing U.S. on Iraq: Deputy Defense Secretary's Interview with CNN Turk," 6 May 2003). The full transcript is available on line at http://usinfo.state.gov/topical/pol/terror/texts/03050706.htm.

DEMOCRACY AND CONFLICT

Jeremy Waldron

While reading Khaled Abou El Fadl's exploration of the prospects for a theory of Islamic democracy, I was struck by the similarity between the way these issues are posed in the Islamic tradition and the way ideas about politics and the rule of law were posed in the context of medieval and early modern thought in the Christian West. There, too, proponents of ideas about law, good governance, individual rights, and consultative decision making had to struggle to make themselves heard in the context of scriptural authority and theocratic rule. And the remarkable thing was that these ideas not only grew up in what appears now to have been a most unpromising environment but were actually energized by religious ideas and ecclesiastical practices. Harold Berman, in his book *Law and Revolution,* has described the role of canon law as a model for the formation of the Western legal tradition, and those who read medieval and early modern theories of natural law know that one of their major contributions was to sustain the idea of the rule of law—paradoxically, the rule of human law—and to limit the pretensions of earthly sovereigns. Religious conceptions of the dignity and basic equality of all those created in God's image also played an indispensable role in the emergence of natural rights.

We can see well enough that Christendom might have nurtured instead doctrines of a closed and implacable authority, of arbitrary bulls and canons presented as decrees from on high, of law as a harsh body of commandments and discipline, of the intolerant suppression of anything that might be deemed heretical, and of the abject subordination of most people under the authority of bishops and kings consecrated with divine right. And God knows there was enough of that. Nevertheless, there turned out to be a way in which ideas at the very foundation of this intolerance and authoritarianism were able to nourish what we can now recognize as the rule of law and human rights. And this should be heartening to those exploring similar possibilities in an adjacent Abrahamic tradition of biblical and potentially theocratic thought.

I say that not as part of a discourse of backwardness and development, as though Islamic thought needs to undergo processes that Christian thought went through five hundred years ago—that would be preposterous as well as insulting. Apart from anything else, it would neglect the role of Islam as a sponsor of Western development, for example in preserving the works of Aristotle and reintroducing them into the Christian West in the twelfth century. Moreover, such a discourse would underrate the role of contingency in all of this. At any stage, the balance of Christian political philosophy might have tilted decisively in favor of authoritarianism (and, for all we can say, it still might). Rather, my point is only that a path was navigated through these obstacles and conundrums. There turned out to be a way of thinking about the rule of law and individual rights that did not involve repudiating the Christian heritage. And if Abou El Fadl is right, Islamic scholars are now exploring a path that is remarkably similar.

As Abou El Fadl notes at the beginning of his essay, liberal constitutionalism, respect for rights, and the rule of law are one site of ideas, but they do not add up to democracy. Democracy depends on the rule of law, to be sure, both for its constitutive procedures and for the respect that its outcomes command (respect for legislation enacted by a representative assembly, for example). But the rule of law can exist without democracy. And the same is true of respect for rights. A society can uphold individual rights (to various liberties, due process, toleration, and guarantees against abuse) without being democratic. There cannot be a democracy without respect for rights, but rights have to have a particular content and flavor before they can help define processes of democratic decision making. I wish Abou El Fadl had drawn these connections more clearly. For example, in a democracy it is not enough that people have rights of free speech or that dissidents are tolerated. In a democracy we have to tolerate dissidents attempting to replace the government. And we have to set up procedures that will allow them to do just that under certain conditions. Toleration may be an admirable human rights ideal, but it is not the same as a principle of loyal opposition, nor is it the same as a system that empowers dissident parties regularly to test the extent of their support in free and fair elections.

For these essentially democratic ideas to emerge in Western thought, it was not sufficient that the rule of law and the dignity of the individual be shown to be compatible with religious foundations. Three additional ideas were necessary: first, the idea that a society was composed of different interests capable of generating diverse perspectives and opinions; second, the idea that when people disagreed about fundamentals, any of the opposed ideas might reasonably become the basis of policy or law; and third, the idea that reasonable controversy might be so pervasive that decisions would have to be taken through processes of deliberation and voting rather than through the individual reflection and pronouncements of an authoritative ruler. It is customary to invoke the Reformation in our account of how these ideas caught on in Christendom, and Abou El Fadl touches on this when he notes "the distinctive context of a post-Reformation, market-oriented Christian Europe." However, I am inclined to think that the role of the Reformation has been exaggerated. Protestant societies are in fact not noted for their acceptance of principles of reasonable disagreement and loyal opposition; often they have been more self-righteously authoritarian than their Catholic counterparts. Instead, what was important in the Judeo-Christian tradition were some older ideas and practices: conciliar decision making within the church; the recognition that people can differ on fundamentals and still regard one another as reasonable, which we see, for example, in Talmudic debate; and above all an awareness that diverse interests in a heterogeneous society are entitled to be heard in their own voice when important political decisions are being made. Abou El Fadl touches on all three points in his article, but more emphasis is needed on each of them in an Islamic theory of democracy. This emphasis would form part of a recognition that the "democracy" we are aiming at is not just a system of constitutional rights but a system of open decision making empowering and facilitating the confrontation between opposed ideas and interests in the context of representation, debate, and voting.

THE BEST HOPE

Noah Feldman

Can Islam and democracy cohere, either in principle or in practice? This crucial question—debated in scores of Arabic books, articles, and *fatwa*s since the temporary success of Islamists in the Algerian elections of 1990—is no longer merely of abstract or regional interest. With the United States poised to invade Iraq, with an announced commitment to establishing a democratic government there, it has become central to American foreign policy. With fair elections in Iraq, some Islamists are bound to win office. And a representative Iraqi constitutional convention must necessarily incorporate the voices of Islamic democrats, committed to the idea that a democratic Iraq should be in some sense an Islamic state. Indeed, the emerging consensus in postwar Afghanistan seems to be that the country ought to be free, democratic, and Islamic. So if "Islamic democracy" is a contradiction in terms, we are in for some very rough times.

It is against this backdrop that one must evaluate the arguments of Khaled Abou El Fadl, a scholar-turned-theologian who has the distinction of being trained both traditionally and academically in Islamic law. Abou El Fadl's hopeful view on the compatibility of democratic values and practices with Islam shares a familial resemblance with the writings of such Islamic democrats as Rashid al-Ghannouchi, a Tunisian Islamist intellectual living in exile in Paris; Abdolkarim Soroush, an Iranian who shuttles between Tehran, Cambridge (Massachusetts), and Princeton; the Egyptian journalist Fahmi Huwaidi; and the Qatar-based internet and al-Jazeera phenomenon Yusuf al-Qaradawi. Though these thinkers disagree on a wide range of issues, they share a view of Islam that emphasizes justice, human dignity and equality, the rule of law, the role of the people in selecting leaders, the obligation of having consultative government, and the value of pluralism. All share a commitment to Islam as the starting place and ultimate ground for evaluating democracy, and all insist that Islam is not self-interpreting: ascertaining the will of God and coordinating quotidian social organization require human effort.

Although Islamic democrats differ in their precise understandings of democracy, they agree that democracy requires much more than elections; it must also incorporate the basic rights necessary to make it both liberal and egalitarian: free speech, free association, freedom of conscience, and equality across race, religion, and gender. Moreover, Islamic democrats find the roots of values such as liberty and equality in Islam—in Qur'anic verses, prophetic Hadith that recount the actions of the Prophet, and Islamic legal tradition. None of these Islamic democrats is prepared for an Islamic state that flouts the authority of Qur'anic verses that seem to have a relatively clear meaning in governing the Muslim community. Thus, for example, Abou El Fadl seems prepared to consider an allegorical reading of the verse requiring the amputation of a thief's hand, and others have suggested that such punishments properly apply only in a Utopian world of perfect distributive equality. But all Islamic democrats face the challenge of grappling with those elements of their tradition that potentially conflict with liberal-democratic commitment.

Efforts such as Abou El Fadl's to synthesize Islam with democracy recall the medieval Islamic philosophers who sought to integrate Aristotle and Plato with an authentically Islamic worldview. Al-Fārābī, Averroës, and Avicenna produced a rich philosophical literature, but their intellectual influence was greater in the Western world, and to a lesser extent the Persian-speaking one, than among the Arabs. The comparison leads to the great question about Islamic democracy: will it work? This question has a theoretical and a practical dimension, each of which deserves a serious answer.

The theoretical undertaking of synthesizing Islam and democracy is promising, but it requires a flexible view of each. It requires acknowledging that democracy, far from being committed to the view that ultimate sovereignty lies with the majority, may in fact depend on nonmajoritarian claims about human liberty and equality. Synthesis also demands an honest recognition that Islam has always developed in a complex interaction with ideas that come from outside, and that the core of divinely revealed Islamic law is relatively small, leaving a tremendous range for reflective political and legal decision making by the demos. Islamic democracy will not emerge spontaneously or as a historical inevitability. But it can emerge as a product of self-conscious efforts by Muslims and others to produce a synthesis that is true to both of its elements.

The practical question of whether Islamic democracy can be made to flourish in the contemporary Muslim world is much dicier. American and Western foreign policy has traditionally supported autocratic regimes in much of the Muslim world, and finding the energy to overcome the inertia of this policy is not easy. The greatest barriers to Islamic democracy now are the autocrats themselves. Dictators and monarchs have repressed the secular and liberal opposition, leaving just enough room for extremist Islamism to tell the West that the only choice is between the autocrats and the radicals. This repression in turn has given the extremists, many of whom are not aspiring democrats, tremendous popular credibility as opponents of unjust regimes.

Still, there is hope for Islamic democracy. Anywhere Islamic democrats have been permitted to run for office, they have done extremely well. In just the last year, Turkey's moderate Islamic democrats in the Justice and Development (AK) Party have formed a government; and the Moroccan party of the same name finished third in Moroccan elections despite being permitted to contest just half of the available seats. In Pakistan, Islamic parties who at least profess some commitment to the democratic process did very well in the recent, flawed elections. Soon Islamic democrats will seek office in a democratic Iraq, and if Afghanistan can become a state at all, it will surely be an Islamic democracy. These experiments carry serious risks: real-world politicians may not share the attractive values and profound sincerity of Khaled Abou El Fadl. But the experiment of Islamic democracy deserves to be run, and the theorists have a role to play in making that happen.

It will be an extraordinary irony if the invasion of Iraq produces an opening for the development of an Islamic democracy; but perhaps only war can dislodge the autocrats who stand in the way. In any case, Muslims and non-Muslims alike should welcome the intellectual efforts and, yes, dreams of Islamic democrats. Born of the enduring appeal of transcendent Islam and the successes of global democracy, their aspirations represent the way of the future. They may not satisfy all Muslims or all democrats. But Islamic democrats are the best hope for the future of the Muslim world—and they deserve our admiration and support.

THE PRIMACY OF POLITICAL PHILOSOPHY

M. A. Muqtedar Khan

THE TYRANNY OF LEGALISM

The Islamic intellectual tradition—which includes Islamic legal thought (*usul al-fiqh* and fiqh), theology (*kalam*), mysticism (*tasawwuf*), and philosophy (*falsafa*)—is highly developed and profound. However, in the area of political philosophy, it remains strikingly underdeveloped. One reason for this is the "colonial" leaning of Islamic legal thought. Many Islamic jurists simply equate Islam with Islamic law (Shariʿah) and privilege the study of the latter. As a result, we have only episodic explorations of the idea of a polity in Islam. Hundreds of Islamic schools and universities now produce hundreds of thousands of legal scholars but hardly any political theorists or philosophers.

With some rare exceptions, this intellectual poverty has reduced Islamic thought to a medieval legal tradition. The extraordinary influence of the idea of Islam as Shariʿah has made law the precursor of the state and political life. Instead of thinking of law as serving the changing needs of the political community, the polity is said to be legitimate only if it properly implements Shari'ah. Abou El Fadl's erudite discussion of the compatibility of Islam and democracy reflects this mistaken view of law and politics. Thus, instead of concluding with a sketch of an Islamic democracy, he imposes Shari'ah-based limitations on democracy.

Abou El Fadl argues that an Islamic democracy should recognize the centrality of Shari'ah in Muslim life. This claim raises several questions. Who gets to articulate what constitutes Shari'ah? Who determines who an Islamic jurist is? Who determines which schools can provide the education that will train jurists? Who determines when a democratically passed law is in violation of Shari'ah? Who determines the issues on which people will have freedom of thought and action and the issues on which the word of the jurists will be unassailable? The answer to all of these questions is the same—the Muslim jurist. A close reading of Abou El Fadl's arguments suggests that an Islamic democracy is essentially a dictatorship of Muslim jurists.

Insisting on the centrality of a fixed Shari'ah is a recipe for authoritarianism. As long as the commanding authority of jurists remains in place and the jurists retain a monopoly on interpretation (Ijtihad), there can be no Islamic democracy. To be sure, the moral quality of this Islamic democracy will depend on the extent of Islamic knowledge and the commitment of its citizens. But attempts to guarantee "Islamic outcomes" by requiring, for example, that "the essential Shari'ah must be applied" will inevitably be subverted. Also, the Prophet of Islam (*pbuh*) reportedly said, "My umma will not unite upon error." But no comparable claim can be made about the infallibility of jurists.

In short, the content of law in an Islamic democracy should be a democratically negotiated conclusion emerging in a democratic society. In the absence of this free and open negotiation, Islamic democracy will be a procedural sham that relegates voting mechanisms to secondary matters.

DIVINE SOVEREIGNTY AND HUMAN AGENCY

The idea that in an Islamic state God is the lawgiver, whereas in a democracy human agents are the source of law, originates with Maulana Maududi, who coined the term *al-hakimiyyah* (sovereignty). He argued that in Islamic states only God is sovereign, whereas in a democracy the will or whim of the majority rules. This misunderstanding of both sovereignty and democracy has become a slogan for Islamists who are opposed to democracy. Democracy implies more than mere majority rule. Constitutional democracies have guarantees that protect individuals from the tyranny of the majority.

Muslims must understand that while sovereignty belongs to God, it has already been delegated in the form of human agency (Qur'an 2:30). To appreciate the nature of this delegation, one has to recognize the difference between sovereignty in principle (*de jure*) and sovereignty in fact (*de facto*). De facto sovereignty is always human whether in a democracy or in an Islamic state. The effect of claiming simply that God is sovereign and has the sole right to legislate is to privilege the few who act in God's name. In an Islamic democracy every individual is a vicegerent of God and therefore has the legitimate authority to act in God's name. Thus every citizen has the right to interpret and claim what is law (divine or otherwise). So we must assume that sovereignty is essentially a human agency that must be both channeled and limited to establish just polities.

Ideas such as the primacy of Shari'ah and God's sovereignty—
which make states accountable to God alone and free them from
accountability to the people—undermine freedom and encour-
age authoritarian states and totalitarian ulema. To establish an Islamic democracy, we must first create a free society in which all
Muslims can debate what constitutes Shari'ah. Freedom comes
first, and only the faith that is found in freedom has any meaning.
The practice of religion under duress violates the Qur'an (2:256).

THE COMPACT OF MEDINA AS A SOCIAL CONTRACT

If we bypass the legalist tradition and return to the original
sources of Islam, we find in the Prophet's example an excellent
model for an Islamic democracy. After Prophet Muhammad
(peace be upon him) migrated from Mecca to Yathrib in 622 C.E.,
he established the first Islamic state on the basis of a tripartite
compact that was signed by the Muhajirun (Muslim immigrants
from Mecca), the Ansar (indigenous Muslims of Medina), and the
Yahud (Jews). This compact established a federation of communities that were equal in rights as well as in duties. The Compact
of Medina provides an excellent historical example of two theoretical constructs that have shaped contemporary democratic
theory—constitutions and social contracts—and should therefore
be of great value to any theoretical reflection on the Islamic state.
It is interesting to note that Abou El Fadl's long essay completely
ignores this very important precedent by Muhammad in favor of
the opinion of jurists.

On the basis of the Compact of Medina, Muhammad ruled Medina by the consent of its citizens and in consultation with them.
The Compact of Medina did not impose Shari'ah on anyone, and

no laws were understood as given *prior* to the compact. Prophet Muhammad's divine mission or the divine message of the Qur'an did not in any way undermine the principles of the compact, though of course the principles enshrined in it echo Islamic principles of equality, consultation, and consent in governance. As long as Islamic jurists focus on the post-Muhammad development in the discipline of Islamic legal thought and privilege it over Muhammad's own practice, authoritarianism will trump democracy in the Muslim milieu.

THE REMAINING CHALLENGES

Democracy must triumph in theory before it can be realized in practice. Muslims must widely and unambiguously accept that Islam and democracy are compatible and that meaningful faith requires freedom. Once we accept these principles, we can address the political issues more easily. But before Muslims can accept democracy as an Islamic principle, Islamic political philosophy must accomplish the following tasks:

1. Link political legitimacy not to the application of a legal code that is prior to politics but to the binding character of shura (consultation).
2. Reject the idea of a fixed Shari'ah in favor of keeping Shari'ah open and dependent on negotiated understandings.
3. Explain how talk of divine sovereignty frees rulers from accountability to the ruled.
4. Acknowledge the limits of the Islamic legal tradition and eschew it in favor of the Compact of Medina as a basis for Islamic democracy.

5. Treat Islam as a fount of values that guide conduct rather than a system of ready-made solutions to problems.

6. Prevent legal opinions from subverting contemporary political reflections. We will be free only when we can freely determine for ourselves what Shari'ah is. There is no mediation in Islam, and the Islamic jurists must step aside. As long as the colonial tendencies of Islamic jurisprudence persist, there will be no Islamic democracy.

THE IMPORTANCE OF CONTEXT

A. Kevin Reinhart

Like many moderns, Khaled Abou El Fadel conceives of Islam as a system, one largely defined in the Islamic legal tradition. He draws from this tradition to advocate democracy; others draw from it to advocate what Malise Ruthven calls Islamo-fascism. (Similarly, Israeli liberals have drawn from the Bible and Jewish values to argue for a liberal democratic state of Israel, and others, like Ovadiah Yosef, argue from the same sources for ethnic cleansing and castelike discrimination. Also, American abolitionists and slavery's apologists alike argued from the Bible.) "Islam and the Challenge of Democracy" should convince those Muslims who believe that democracy can only be an alien ideology in Islamdom and those Westerners who think that Islam precludes Muslims from participating in an authentic liberal democracy.

But is Islam a system, and is its political philosophy derived from Islamic law? I think the ethnographer or historian would have to part company with the Muslim legal-political philosopher. Only in the twentieth century—perhaps only since the 1930s— has Islam been conceived of as a self-subsistent "system." Even Islamic jurists in the premodern period recognized that government included administrative rules with no religious content or grounding. Furthermore, Muslim ideals have been shaped as much by Persian and Greek political and philosophical ideas as by Muslim ones. When even a jurist like al-Ghazali writes about governing, he explicitly and implicitly draws on non-Islamic sources and notions of why we have government and what good government requires. An "Islamic democracy" need not be justified solely in Islamic terms.

Islam is a repertoire, not a schema. Even in its own terms Islam is and has always been multivalent. It is hard to think of a religious tradition that has, as a matter of religious doctrine, made a larger space for difference—"In difference is mercy," as the Prophet's Hadith declares. Within the Sunni denomination are four schools of law, seven or fourteen acceptable recitations of the Qur'an, six canonical works of the Hadith, and so forth. So when someone refers to Islam (which is challenged by democracy), a historian asks first, "Which Islam?" Of course, Muslims have to choose among the various Islamic possibilities. For the ethnographer or historian, the question is not What is Islam? but Which Islam have Muslims chosen to construct?

As Mary Douglas has pointed out, institutions are pertinent to the social and economic conditions within which they exist. Incongruent institutions, like ideas, wither and disappear. So it is not enough that Abou El Fadl provides a smart reading of Islamic legal-political theory, one that finds the essence of democracy in Islam. The "practical hurdles that democracy faces in Islamic countries," as he writes, cannot be ignored when we assess the persuasiveness of Abou El Fadl's arguments about Islamic democracy. For instance, if the people invading, ignoring, or otherwise intruding on Muslim lands and cultures deploy Abou El Fadl's arguments to justify their actions, these arguments become stigmatized by association with the wrong being done to Muslims. If defense, resistance, or self-assertion seems to be the most urgent demand of the moment, the Qur'anic emphases on justice and mercy central to Abou El Fadl's argument will be displaced by other Qur'anic texts urging Muslims to protect themselves and to resist and defeat an externally imposed tyranny. Muslims will choose whether democracy is an Islamic form of government, and not just on the basis of which side has the most or best texts. In other words, while Abou El Fadl's enterprise is essential for democracy in Islamdom, it is not sufficient. His *Speaking in God's Name* and *The Authoritative and Authoritarian in Islamic Discourses* are ur-texts for an Islamic alternative to obscurantist and fundamentalist Islamic politics, but the actual effect of his arguments is hostage to forces he does not control.

I have to confess, however, that I liked the essay and found his reorientation of the tradition rigorous yet never polemically dishonest to the sources. Still, I was struck by the essay's asymmetry. So much of comparative ethics or politics takes for granted the perfected state of liberal Western politics, or at least political theory. All that's left for the comparativist is to find, amid the slag of other traditions, nuggets to be refined and molded into a faithful image of Western notions and practices. Is there nothing for us to learn from the comparison, or is comparison mostly an act of missionary charity?

Obviously I think there is something to be learned besides how special we are. One point in Abou El Fadl's essay is suggestive, and perhaps it is worth pointing to. Toward the end of his essay, Abou El Fadl discusses the notion of democratic rights. He believes this has an Islamic analogue in the concept of *haqq* (pl. *huquq*). He rightly rejects the idea that Islamic ethics is an ethics only of duties, or is collectivist and not individualist in orientation. Yet by trying to shoehorn the European terms *droit, rights,* and *Recht* into *haqq,* he impoverishes the discussion. If we understand *haqq* as "right," we get confusing notions like "the rights of God"—what could that mean? I think it is not quite correct to say that a haqq arises "from a legal cause brought about by the suffering of a legal wrong." In Islamic law, the term is better understood simply as "(justified) claim." A claim arises when one is in the right, proleptically or after some legal fact. God does not suffer when someone commits felony theft, but the sanction is God's claim against the thief for his or her transgression. (The victim, of course, also has a claim for the recovery of the stolen property.)

The fact is, ordinarily we tend to use the term *right* without noticing that a right requires a surrender of something by someone else—whether it is power, freedom to act, or something more tangible. Human rights are claims that require states or governments to restrict their power over the actions and bodies of individual subjects, just as my right of way requires that you yield your right to proceed. The phrase "rights of the Palestinians" is not just an abstract appeal for nice things to happen to them but claims against a state, or states, that require limiting or surrendering the capacity that raw military power otherwise gives them. Clichéd doublets that are regularly invoked—"right to work," "women's rights," "right to life (of the fetus)," "right to choose (by a woman)"—are claims against someone or something. They have costs. There is something almost retributive about rights when considered in their social context. And my point is only that when we enter into the comparative discussion honestly, we can, in this instance, learn about "our" conceptual world (and perhaps be corrected or enlightened in the process) as well as "theirs."

So yes, at a theoretical level a democratic system could be authentically Islamic as well as democratic—if circumstances permit. Whether they permit it is not entirely in the hands of Muslims—or at least Muslims like Khaled Abou El Fadl. It is doubtful whether evolving Muslim ideas of democracy will be or need to be constructed only from Islamic sources. In addition, it is also worth wondering more radically whether liberal democracies and their proponents are liberal enough to learn from, among others, Muslims.

IS LIBERALISM ISLAM'S ONLY ANSWER?

Saba Mahmood

◈ Khaled Abou El Fadl's essay is an erudite attempt to explore those principles and values within Islamic political and legal traditions that could be made compatible with ideas of liberal democracy. Abou El Fadl joins a growing number of scholars who have been writing on this theme in the last three decades; some of these writers are in the Muslim world and others in Europe and the United States. These thinkers represent a wide spectrum of political perspectives: some support the reformist trend within the Islamist movement (for example, Tariq al-Bishri in Egypt, the Tunisian scholar Rashid al-Ghannouchi, who lives in exile in France, and Abdolkarim Soroush in Iran), and others espouse a more straightforward secular-liberal line (such as Said Ashmawi in Egypt, Nurcholish Madjid in Indonesia, and Aziza al-Hibri in the United States). The increased attention that the Western media have recently given to these explorations is an indication of the hope that "liberal Islam" has been invested with—following the events of September 11—a potential resource for "saving Islam" from its more militant and fundamentalist interpreters.

Curiously, in these explorations by Muslim scholars, Islam bears the burden of proving its compatibility with liberal ideals, and the line of question is almost never reversed. We do not ask, for example, What would it mean to take the resources of the Islamic tradition and question many of the liberal political categories and principles for the contradictions and problems they embody? Or, how would one rethink these problems by bringing the resources of Islamic political history to bear upon them? For instance, many of the aforementioned authors, including Khaled Abou El Fadl, urge that liberal conceptions of individual autonomy, human rights, and individual freedom be incorporated into Islam. Thus Abou El Fadl, in his essay, argues that the "Qur'anic celebration and sanctification of human diversity" should be made the ground for incorporating what appears to be a liberal conception of tolerance: "an ethic that respects dissent and honors . . . the right to adhere to different religious or nonreligious convictions." It is striking that the normative claims of liberal conceptions such as tolerance are taken at face value, and no attention is paid to the contradictions, struggles, and problems that these ideals actually embody. As scholars of liberalism have shown, the historical trajectory of a concept like tolerance encompasses violent struggles that dispossessed peoples have had to wage to be considered legitimate members of liberal societies—not to mention the ongoing battles about what it means to tolerate someone or something, who does the tolerating and who is tolerated, under what circumstances, and toward what end. Given this fraught history, is it not worth pausing to reflect whether other traditions, such as Islam, might have their own resources for imagining "an ethic that respects dissent and honors the right . . . to adhere to different religious or nonreligious convictions"?

Different conceptions of religious and communal coexistence, for example, informed the social and political life of the diverse communities that lived under the Ottoman Empire and even under Mughal rule in South Asia. These conceptions were not organized around the problem of majority and minority populations. In the Ottoman system, for instance, non-Muslim communities were vertically integrated into a hierarchical ruling structure but had their own independent legal systems. This mutual accommodation enabled different social groups living under a shared political structure to practice distinct ways of life; life-worlds were the preconditions for an individual's existence, rather than the objects of individual interests as they are conceived within liberal democratic thought. The system did not make non-Muslims the social or legal equals of Muslims, but it did grant them a certain autonomy to practice and develop their traditions in a manner that is almost inconceivable under the present system of nation-states. The reason I bring up this different understanding of coexistence is not because I believe in its moral superiority or consider it an example from the Islamic tradition that could be made commensurable with a liberal understanding of tolerance. Rather, I want to use this history to ask what I think is a far more interesting set of questions, such as: how does this history make us rethink the politics of tolerance and pluralism beyond the confines of individualism to include the rights of plural social groupings? Or, for that matter, to ask whether the liberal meaning of tolerance is the best or the most desirable one; what does this understanding preclude, under what kinds of presuppositions, and for whom?

I believe that the reason these kinds of questions are seldom pursued is the hegemony that liberalism commands as a political ideal for many contemporary Muslim intellectuals, a hegemony that reflects the enormous disparity in power between the Anglo-European countries and what constitutes the Muslim world today. Indeed, the idea that the liberal political system is the best arrangement for all human societies, regardless of their diverse histories and conceptual and material resources, is rarely questioned these days. One would think that the proponents of pluralism and diversity, such as Abou El Fadl, would want to explore some of the contrasting ways in which questions of difference have been imagined and politically instituted within different nonliberal traditions.

Abou El Fadl's essay is largely a philosophical exercise, one that does not take into account the practical impediments to the institutionalization of democracy in the Muslim world. Had he been concerned with practical issues, he would have had to deal with complicated questions such as why some of the worst violations of democracy in the name of Islam have been perpetrated by states (for example, Saudi Arabia, Kuwait, and Pakistan) that have been propped up by liberal democracies like the United States—support without which these states would not have survived in their present form. A more practical engagement would also have had to deal with the fact that the problems of religious and ethnic strife, or the abrogation of democratic freedoms, do not simply reflect the "undemocratic" tendencies within Islam but characterize most secular regimes in the Third World today. As many scholars have recently taught us, these problems are not unrelated to the liberal forms of government implemented by colonial and postcolonial states. I do not fault Abou El Fadl for his philosophical inquiry. But what I do find problematic is his failure to subject to critical scrutiny our liberal notions of justice, autonomy, tolerance, individual rights, and so on, from the standpoint of the Islamic traditions he so clearly holds dear. Rather than ask the question of how Muslims can become better liberals, it is far more pressing to ask how the world is (or can be) lived differently—confronted as we are with a historically unprecedented homogenizing force of modernity that will brook no arguments for an alternative vision.

POPULAR SUPPORT FIRST

Bernard Haykel

Khaled Abou El Fadl is one of the most accomplished liberal Muslim legal scholars of our time. His present article argues for the compatibility of Islam and democracy on the basis that both are premised on, and aim for, the same fundamental moral value: the pursuit of justice, which entails guaranteeing human dignity and liberty. Abou El Fadl's argument is ultimately centered on the establishment of a set of moral and ethical claims that are anchored more in theology than in law. In so doing, he appears to argue for a suspension of the injunctions that are constitutive of an Islamic legal order by claiming Shariʿah to be a hyper-phenomenon not fully comprehensible by people and therefore not completely enforceable. As such, he is able to interpret away certain texts of revelation that at face value seem to clash with democratic ideals. Abou El Fadl's ideas are intensely stimulating and innovative and point to the fact that Muslims in the West are playing an increasingly important role in global Islamic political and intellectual life. Having said this, I find missing from his analysis the actual processes and mechanisms, both legal and extralegal, that might help bring about the desired reconciliation. I would therefore like to raise one or two issues that might address these lacunae and thereby further strengthen his case.

Let us consider slavery. Modern Muslims, other than a minority in the Sudan and Mauritania, roundly condemn the institution despite the fact that it is part of Islamic law. Evidence of its unacceptability can be gleaned from a recently translated and much-quoted medieval Islamic legal manual, "The Reliance of the Traveler," in which the modern translator does not provide an English translation of the laws pertaining to slaves. Another example is that modern Muslims have ceased to expound, in writing or in sermons, on these laws. One might therefore argue that a universal Islamic consensus, not merely of the jurists but of each and every Muslim, obtains at present, and this makes slavery illegal in Islam forever. The basis for this consensus can be argued to be reason (ʿaql) or even inspiration (ilham), and in either case one will find premodern authorities to back such an argument. Moreover, the law forbidding slavery would hold even if the claim to a universal consensus proves to be a legal fiction (as all arguments about consensus tend to be) because some group of strict constructionists (for example, Salafis) would steadfastly insist that slavery is a private entitlement that can never be revoked. What ultimately decides the matter is the force of mass adherence to the principle that slavery is illegal, and this renders it so. Through this, the Prophet's statement "my community shall not agree upon an error" acquires renewed significance.

The question of democracy is in a number of respects analogous to slavery. First, the institution of the supreme leadership of the Muslim community, otherwise known as the caliphate, has fallen into abeyance since at least 1924, when the Turkish Republic deposed the last self-styled caliph. Some Islamist groups claim to want to reestablish the post, but their discussions lack rigor, are desultory, and thus far have no wide appeal. In addition, many leading scholars in both the Sunni and Shi'ite communities (for example, Yusuf al-Qaradawi and Mohsen Kadivar, to name but two) declare Islam and democracy to be compatible and argue that the Muslim ruler must be understood as a servant of the people (*ajir*) who is elected for a fixed term of office. Arab countries have yet to experience democracy in any real and sustained sense, and little more than anecdotal evidence can be relayed about their populations' desire for it—though I have no doubt they do. The experience in Turkey, and in some respects in Iran, leads one to think that Muslims in both countries perceive democracy as not only being compatible with their beliefs but as a necessary aspect of political life, one that protects them from tyranny. Even the so-called hard-liners in Iran are unable to stop the democratic process in their country, despite severe attempts at curtailing it through the Council of Guardians. In short, if sufficient numbers of Muslims deem democracy to be constitutive of their religion and institutionalize its processes, the question of the compatibility of Islam and democracy will become moot.

I look forward to the day when Muslim students look as perplexed when I mention that Muslim jurists once argued that despotism, as a necessary evil, is an acceptable form of government as they do now when I mention the laws of slavery in Islam.

TOO FAR FROM TRADITION

Mohammad H. Fadel

Khaled Abou El Fadl argues passionately that democracy and Islam share certain fundamental moral tenets, and that Muslims may therefore assimilate democratic norms without abandoning their religious beliefs. He marshals an impressive array of sources in support of his argument: verses from the Qur'an and the sayings of the Prophet Muhammad, as well as medieval works of Islamic jurisprudence, treatises of Islamic substantive and constitutional law, and Islamic political philosophy. The sheer breadth of his argument precludes a detailed response here, and, accordingly, I address only some of the major points of his argument.

1. Abou El Fadl insists that democracy and Islam must be understood as "moral systems." The affinity of Islam and democracy lies in the concept of justice: democracy is a system of government that "offers the greatest potential for promoting justice and protecting human dignity." Abou El Fadl argues that because Islam is widely acknowledged to be concerned with justice, "justice" is the "key" moral value by which the moral systems of democracy and Islam should interact.

But Abou El Fadl also points to a fundamental tension within the Islamic tradition: does justice exist independently of the norms of revelation, or is justice itself known only as a consequence of revelation? Unlike Abou El Fadl, most Muslim theologians settled on the latter position—that knowledge of what is just and good requires revelation. This position was not necessarily an indictment of human reason, which could, according to these same theologians, be relied on to demonstrate the existence of God and distinguish truth from falsehood. Rather, it was a recognition that because the ultimate good is salvation and not justice (understood as a matter of how we interact with one another, and not as a matter of right conduct generally or of submitting oneself and one's desires to the rule of reason), revelation has priority in issues of moral knowledge. It is somewhat surprising, then, that Abou El Fadl would partly ground the basis for democratic life among Muslims on a heretofore discredited theological argument, according to which justice is independent of relevation. His case would have been stronger if he had demonstrated that democracy is consistent with either theory of the good traditionally espoused by Muslim theologians.

2. Abou El Fadl's focus on the relationship of justice to revelation also obscures some fundamental points about Islamic law. Islamic law is not simply derived from revelation; nor is it merely scriptural exegesis. Much of Islamic law, as Muslim jurists understand it, is conventional. That is the case with rules of international law. In other areas, such as contract law, Islamic law provides a set of procedures that regulates the exchange of entitlements created by some other system—for example, property law. Accordingly, one can accept the orthodox theological position that revelation

defines the good, at the same time acknowledging that revelation answers only a limited number of cases. So the application of revealed principles requires human societies and conventions to establish baseline entitlements. How those entitlements are to be distributed requires some theory of the state and justice, even if only implicit.

Thus the Qur'an provides that, as a religious matter, a man may marry up to four wives simultaneously. Viewed from the perspective of salvation, then, plural marriage is not sinful. But revelation does not answer the legal question of whether, as a default matter, men should have an entitlement to multiple marriages, and if so, whether such an entitlement should be alienable or inalienable. These matters depend on social convention. This approach to Islamic law mirrors two terms used by the Qur'an for justice, *'adl* and *ma'ruf,* the former denoting procedural justice and the latter meaning substantive justice. Significantly, the latter term literally means "that which is known" and thus suggests conventional (and hence) changing norms.

3. Abou El Fadl's argument fails to address why, if the ultimate good is salvation, a Muslim should prefer a democratic state to a theocratic regime that teaches true doctrine. Medieval scholastic theology, which declared that the first moral obligation of a human being is inquiry, may provide a solid basis to explore this question: democracy permits members to fulfill that first obligation, whereas a theocratic regime does not. One could also point to the historical distaste exhibited by (at least) Sunni Muslims for regimes claiming infallible access to metaphysical truths as another factor privileging democratic life over life in an authoritarian regime. Finally, the well-established theological principle that human

culpability before God arises only after an individual has had a sufficient opportunity to discover and reflect on the proofs of God's unicity and the truth of the prophets' messages also provides a theological justification of diversity, by allowing for the possibility that persons may earn salvation, regardless of their belief, if they spend their lives diligently pursuing truth.

4. Abou El Fadl aims to show that the Qur'an can be read to support democracy. But that does not go far enough. One must also show that fundamental principles of the Islamic tradition reinforce the notion of a democratic society and that such principles outweigh other readings that appear to contradict democratic notions. Abou El Fadl's argument is weakest on this point. He pursues what some constitutional scholars might call a top-down approach, whereby one begins with abstract values (whether legal or religious/moral) and then, based on those values, establishes the rules of a society. I advocate a bottom-up approach, whereby one begins with well-established legal rules, moral principles, and theological truths to demonstrate that these rules, principles, and truths, taken as a whole, are more consistent with a democratic society than an authoritarian one.

Consider the case of human autonomy. Muslims may favor human autonomy as a political matter, not because of an abstract commitment to human dignity[1] but because human autonomy is a requirement of living a moral life and thus is necessary for salvation. Muslims' commitment to individual autonomy can be easily demonstrated by citing numerous well-known medieval authors as well as substantive rules that protect autonomy.[2] On this bottom-up approach, autonomy is deeply rooted in a wide range of rules and practices, not in a single value treated as a basic moral axiom.

5. Abou El Fadl argues, surprisingly, that the notion of enforcing God's law is logically incoherent. Islamic law is indeterminate, he writes. And he concludes that when its rules are enforced coercively, it is not the rule of God that is vindicated but rather "the state's law." The same objection can be raised against a secular legal system that derives its coercive legitimacy from the notion that it is enforcing the sovereign will of the people. Certainly the popular will is at least as indeterminate and subject to manipulation as revealed law. Does that mean that American judges, for example, enforce only their subjective notions of the law, and that the rule of law, because it is mediated by the subjective agency of fallible (and perhaps fickle) judges, conflicts with democratic ideals? Alternatively, one might argue that the language of revelation is particularly opaque in contrast to legislative statutes and judicial opinions. Such an argument would not garner much support among Muslims, however, because revelation, whether Qur'anic or in the form of Prophetic sayings, has always been deemed to be a model of literary excellence and clarity.

So Abou El Fadl's argument suggests that no system of adjudication can effectively vindicate a moral vision, in which case, we are left with the question, Under what conditions are the coercive powers of the state legitimate? Although Abou El Fadl has suggested possible answers from the perspective of a Muslim liberal—in particular, that democracy provides a basis for legitimate law—his answers raise their own difficult questions. I am convinced that the majority of Muslim intellectuals are, like me, persuaded of the truth of Abou El Fadl's conclusions. What is still open to debate, however, is whether his specific arguments for democracy are convincing in Islamic terms.

NOTES

1. For example, the Qur'an states, "We have indeed created man in the most handsome of forms, then we reduced him to the lowest of the low, save for those who believe [in God] and perform good deeds."

2. For example, a famous medieval Mamluk jurist, al-ʿIzz b. ʿAbd al-Salam, noted in one of his works of jurisprudence that interference with the autonomy of a free person is a legal injury that can be justified only in limited circumstances.

REVEALED LAW AND DEMOCRACY

David Novak

🔲 As a non-Muslim, and one having a superficial knowledge of
Islam, it would be inappropriate for me to evaluate the Islamic validity of Khaled Abou El Fadl's argument for the possibility of an Is-
lamic-democratic regime, that is, an Islamic regime that could in
good faith and with rational cogency incorporate much of what
more and more people in the world regard to be the desideratum
of modern democracy. Nevertheless, as a Jew who very much
wants to live with Muslims in a peace based on mutual respect, I
am indeed interested in Abou El Fadl's project. It is very attractive,
if only from afar. Although, for reasons of faith and knowledge—
being an adherent of Judaism, a religion that, like Islam, bases itself
on a divinely revealed law—I cannot enter into Abou El Fadl's di-
alectic, I can certainly understand his problematic and thus mutatis
mutandis see something very similar to it within Judaism. Moreover, like Abou El Fadl as a Muslim, I as a Jew want to live in a democratic regime in good faith and with rational cogency. Finally, I
believe that the lethal political problems between Muslims and
Jews admit a solution only if Muslims and Jews can find similar
ways to deal with their respective theological-political problems.
Today, that means finding similar ways to participate in democratic

regimes without, however, regarding democracy as having super-
seded either Islam or Judaism, both of which certainly transcend
any democracy in the existential claims they make. In this political
context, thinking analogically might provide a modus vivendi for a
fruitful Muslim-Jewish dialogue now and in the future.

In his very rich and suggestive essay, Abou El Fadl presents two
antinomies, which could just as well apply to Judaism. First, there
is the antinomy between the divine authority of revealed law and
the human authority of popular sovereignty. If God exercises authority, what need is there for human authority? If humans exercise authority, what need is there for divine authority? Second,
there is the antinomy between general justice and specific law. If
justice precedes law, what need is there for law at all? If law precedes justice, what need is there for justice at all? I am convinced
that these two antinomies are in essence one, so that the solution
of one is the solution of the other.

The antinomy between divine authority and human authority is
irreconcilable only if one assumes that democracy as a desideratum is grounded in human authority, that is, that the people are
sovereign absolutely. However, democracy grounded in human
authority is the rule of a human collective, a demos, what we
would today call a mob. Now, if the principled protection of the
prior rights of human persons is the chief desideratum of democracy—that is, constitutional democracy—then a mob (no matter
how orderly) is in no position to offer any such protection, let
alone encouragement. At best, these rights can be postulated only
as social entitlements by utilitarian criteria, and, as such, they can
be rescinded quite easily at will by employing those same utilitarian criteria. So, it would seem—and the American experience of
democracy provides the best paradigm—rights as democracy's
chief desideratum are most cogently grounded when seen as God-

given entitlements or endowments to human persons created in
God's image (what I think Abou El Fadl, basing himself on the
Qur'an, would call the viceroys of God on this earth). These rights
are irrevocable by any human authority—and, maybe, even by
God Himself. Furthermore, these rights provide the very reason a
civil society like a democracy is instituted *ab initio*. Thus the very
purpose of any humanly founded collective or polity is to implement these divinely given human rights, which are beyond its
authority to either give or take away. That is why, in the end, religious justifications of democracy turn out to be more rationally
persuasive than competing secularist justifications of it.

To accept this solution of the antinomy between divine authority and human authority, though, one has to accept the notion that
there are two divine laws, or better, two distinct aspects of one divine law. The divine law being assumed in the solution of this first
antinomy is what some Jewish theologians have called the rational
commandments (*mitsvot sikhliyot*). They are that aspect of the
law of God which can be understood by rational reflection on
human nature per se as a permanent set of relations between humans and God and between humans themselves. And that can be
understood without (or better, before) any specific revelation to
certain people. This aspect of the law of God is most cogently formulated through philosophy. Nevertheless, it is not what constitutes the concrete norms by which faithful Jews actually live.
Those concrete norms are what some Jewish theologians have
called the revealed commandments (*mitsvot shimiyot*). They are
contained in the Torah and are structured in a system called *halakhah*. (One could say that in Judaism the Torah functions like
Shari'ah does in Islam, and halakhah functions like fiqh.)

This leads us to Abou El Fadl's second antinomy: If justice, why
law? Or if law, why justice? (Philosophers will recognize this as

the same question Socrates asked the Athenian pietist Euthyphro in Plato's dialogue by that name.) For a solution, we must see how justice and law, reason and revelation, are to be ordered together. This requires an understanding of three kinds of priority: (1) ontological, (2) historical, and (3) logical.

For any Jew to assume that general justice is ontologically prior to specifically revealed law is to subordinate theology to philosophy. In the modern world, this has meant that religion has had to justify itself by its ethical value alone. Thus the relationship with God, the subject of theology, has been subordinated to interhuman relationships, the subject of (in Kant's important term) practical philosophy. As for historical priority, the modern notion of history as a progressive trajectory from a particularistic past into a more universal future gives the future historical priority over the past. Particularistic religion is to prepare us for universal ethics. But in modern times, this has led to the thorough undermining of the unique authority of halakhah, which was most pervasive in the success of Reform Judaism and its liberal offspring. I cannot imagine that Abou El Fadl would want a similarly liberal approach for contemporary Islam. It has not been very good for the Jewish tradition.

Nevertheless, one can assert the logical and historical priority of general justice over specifically revealed divine law, but without falling into the liberal trap of ontologically reducing theology to philosophy, which has been perpetuated on Judaism by Jewish religious liberals. Furthermore, one need not fall into the liberal illusion of historical progress.

Historically, Judaism has taught that *before* the Jews accepted God's law specially revealed to them on Mount Sinai, they had been living under a general law (called the commandments for the children of Noah), one they shared with all humankind. Moreover, the general law was not abrogated by the Jews' acceptance of the special revelation, neither for the Jews nor for the gentiles. Rather, its universalizable norms were incorporated into the new, specific, revealed law. And, in fact, one can see in this type of normative universalizability what is needed to properly ground a rights-based constitutional democracy, that is, a democratic society with a republican form of government.

Because the general divine law was not abrogated by specific revelation, it can have a logical priority to that specifically revealed law as well. That logical priority functions as the human precondition of revelation. That is, specific revelation and its special law can be accepted by intelligent and free persons only if it is presented as the law of the One God who created the world and rules it by His law. The revealed law is meant to be the more intense version of that overall divine law, the version that constitutes a direct relationship of a human community with God, a relationship that is impossible through general justice alone. But, if at least one human community did not accept the general law of God as creator or king, there would be nobody in a position to accept the more intense version of this law. Indeed, at the deepest level, one can understand the quest for humanly effected justice as leading to the quest for direct divine revelation. Respect for humans created in the image of God leads one to desire a direct presentation of the God behind that image, the God who cast it.

Because of this logical priority—what makes human acceptance of divine revelation possible as an intelligent free choice—these universalizable norms of earthly justice function as ever-present criteria whereby revealed law is rationally interpreted and applied. This is what enables the revealed law to retain its essential rationality. It is also what prevents revealed law's distortion by fanatics of various sorts and its becoming the tyrannical tool of oligarchies, be they clerical or secular. Yet all this does not mean that from universalizable norms of justice one must or even can deduce the greater richness and sanctity of the revealed law of the Torah. Justice, especially as philosophically formulated, *informs* the interpretation and application of divinely revealed law. Yet it does not ground it. In the same way, democratic experience and philosophical reflection thereon can guide—though not govern—the interpretation and application of normative Judaism. And this can be done without in any way subordinating the law of God to human autonomy. Both divine authority and human authority are needed in proper order, and both revealed law and justice are also needed in proper order.

These questions of revelation and reason, raised so well by Abou El Fadl, are the perennial concerns of Muslims, Christians, and Jews, namely, all who live by a law that God has revealed to them respectively. The analogies between these three traditions of revelation are not accidental, and they are of great importance for the world in which Muslims, Christians, and Jews—and all others—have to live and want to flourish.

PRACTICE AND THEORY

John L. Esposito

▣ Many people charge that both the religion of Islam and the realities of Muslim politics demonstrate that Islam is incompatible with democracy. Across the political and ideological spectrum, the Muslim experience has been one of kings, military rulers, and ex-military rulers possessing tenuous legitimacy and propped up by military and security forces. In Syria the president's son recently succeeded his father; and some believe the rulers of Libya, Egypt, and Iraq now entertain such a possibility. Some Islamic governments—the Taliban's Afghanistan, Saudi Arabia, Iran, and Sudan—have projected a religiously based authoritarianism that parallels secular authoritarianism. And since September 11, many Muslim governments have used the threat of global terrorism as an excuse or a green light for increasing their authoritarian rule.

At the same time, while much of the world has focused on the threat from extremist Islamic organizations, mainstream Islamic candidates and parties have continued to participate in the political process, performing impressively in the 2002 elections in Morocco, Bahrain, Pakistan, and Turkey, where the Justice and Development (AK) Party came to power.

Questions about the compatibility of Islam and democracy have, then, been contentious issues in recent decades among rulers, policymakers, religious scholars (ulema), Islamic activists (Islamists or fundamentalists), and intellectuals in the Muslim world and the West. And these questions have grown in importance in recent decades, as diverse sectors of society—secular and religious, leftist and rightist, educated and uneducated—have increasingly used democratization as a basis for judging the legitimacy of governments and political movements. In the late 1980s and 1990s, responding to failed economies and public unrest (food riots in Egypt, Algeria, Tunisia, and Jordan) and to calls for democratization that accompanied the breakup of the Soviet Union, governments hesitantly opened their systems and held limited elections. Islamic activists and parties emerged as the leading opposition and were poised to come to power in Algeria (1991-1992) after sweeping parliamentary elections. Stunned, many governments and experts in the Muslim world and the West, after a decade of charging that Islamic movements did not enjoy significant popular support and would be turned away in elections, were quick to warn that Islamic movements threatened to hijack democracy.

Closer to home, many conservatives—who during the Cold War promoted relations with authoritarian regimes in Latin America, Africa, and the Middle East in the name of America's national interest—have also questioned Islam's compatibility with democracy. But even here, things are complicated. Secretary of State Colin Powell, speaking for the Bush administration in the spring of 2003, embraced democratization in the Muslim world as part of America's agenda in the war against global terrorism. In an interview, Powell went out of his way not to rule out U.S. support for Islamic parties. At the time of Turkey's election and the AK Party victory, he noted: "The fact that the party has an Islamic base to it in and of itself does not mean that it will be anti-American in any way. In fact, the initial indication we get is that the new party, which forms the new government, understands the importance of a good relationship with the United States."[1]

So, are Islam and democracy compatible? In addressing this question, we need to start with a general observation: religious traditions are a combination of text and context—revelation and human interpretation within a specific sociohistorical context. All religious traditions demonstrate dynamism and diversity, which is why there are conservative as well as modernist or progressive elements in all religions. Judaism and Christianity, the Hebrew Bible and the New Testament, have been used to legitimize monarchies and feudalism in the past and democracy and capitalism, as well as socialism, in the present. The Gospels and Christianity have been used to legitimize the accumulation of wealth and market capitalism as well as religiosocial movements like those of Francis of Assisi and in the twentieth century Dorothy Day's Catholic Worker Movement and Liberation Theology in Latin and Central America. Moreover, democracy itself has meant different things to different peoples at different times, from ancient Greece to modern Europe, from direct to indirect democracy, from majority rule to majority vote. Can Islam travel a similar path?

Generally speaking, the answer seems to be yes. Throughout history, Islam has proven dynamic and diverse. It has adapted to support the movement from the city-state of Medina to empires and sultanates; it was also able to encompass diverse schools of theology, law, and philosophy as well as different Sunni and Shi'i branches; and it has been used to support both extremism and conservative orthodoxy. Islam continues to lend itself to multiple interpretations of government; it is used to support limited democracy and dictatorship, republicanism and monarchy. Like other religions, Islam possesses intellectual and ideological resources that can provide the justification for a wide range of political models.

With respect to democracy in particular, a diversity of voices within the Islamic world are now debating issues of political participation. Secularists argue for the separation of religion and state. Rejectionists (both moderate and militant Muslims) maintain that Islam's forms of governance do not conform to democracy. King Fahd of Saudi Arabia says that "the democratic system prevalent in the world is not appropriate in this region. . . . The election system has no place in the Islamic creed, which calls for a government of advice and consultation and for the shepherd's openness to his flock, and holds the ruler fully responsible before his people."[2] Extremists agree, condemning any form of democracy as *haram*, or forbidden, an idolatrous threat to God's rule (divine sovereignty). Their unholy wars aim to topple governments and impose an authoritarian Islamic rule. Conservatives often argue that popular sovereignty contradicts the sovereignty of God, with the result that the alternative has often been some form of monarchy.

Modern reformers in the twentieth century began to reinterpret key traditional Islamic concepts and institutions—rulers' consultation (shura) with those ruled, consensus (*ijma*) of the community, reinterpretation (ijtihad), and legal principles such as the public welfare (*maslaha*)—to develop Islamic forms of parliamentary governance, representative elections, and religious reform. Reformers in the twenty-first century, like Khaled Abou El Fadl, continue the process in diverse ways.

Some advocates of Islamic democracy argue that the doctrine of the Oneness of God (*tawhid*), or monotheism, requires some form of democratic system. "No Muslim questions the sovereignty of God or the rule of Shariʿah, Islamic law. However, most Muslims do (and did) have misgivings about any claims by one person that he is sovereign. The sovereignty of one man contradicts the sovereignty of God, for all men are equal in front of God. . . . Blind obedience to [a] one-man rule is contrary to Islam."[3]

However, reformist efforts toward political liberalization, electoral politics, and democratization in the Muslim world do not imply uncritical acceptance of Western democratic forms. Many Muslims observe that legitimate democracy can take many forms. President Mohammad Khatami, in a June 2001 television interview before the Iranian presidential elections, noted that "the existing democracies do not necessarily follow one formula or aspect. It is possible that a democracy may lead to a liberal system . . . [or] to a socialist system. Or it may be a democracy with the inclusion of religious norms in the government. We have accepted the third option." According to Khatami, "[W]orld democracies are suffering from a . . . vacuum of spirituality," and Islam can provide the framework for combining democracy with spirituality and religious government.

Like changes in other faiths, shifts in Islamic religious thought will be a slow process as the meaning of sacred texts, doctrines, and traditions is examined and debated. The players continue to differ on many critical questions and issues: the relationship of divine sovereignty to human sovereignty, the nature of Islamic government, the relationship between ruler and ruled, the role of law, individual rights, and pluralism. Perhaps the most critical and explosive issue has been Shariʿah and associated issues of divine versus human sovereignty and divine law versus human legislation. The implementation of Shariʿah—or perhaps more accurately the claims to having implemented Shariʿah law—have wreaked havoc and led to grave injustices in some Muslim countries in matters affecting women and non-Muslims as well as Muslims. Too often Shariʿah is simply (and incorrectly) equated by Muslims and non-Muslims alike with Islamic law, the body of laws developed by Muslim jurists in the past and/or implemented by some governments.

In "Islam and the Challenge of Democracy," Abou El Fadl addresses the heart of this issue. He notes that "for the most part, Shariʿah is not explicitly dictated by God. Rather, it relies on the interpretive act of the human agent for its production and execution." He makes the critical distinction between Shariʿah, with its normative revealed principles, values and legal rules, and fiqh, its human interpretation, production, and application, which are historically and socially conditioned. This distinction underscores the relative, fallible human dimension of Islamic law as well as its dynamic nature, which enables it to respond to multiple and diverse situations. Many reformers since the late nineteenth century have expressed the divine-human, immutable-mutable dimensions of Islamic law by distinguishing duties to God (*ibadat*)—worship, unchanging religious observances such as praying five times a day, the fast of Ramadan, and pilgrimage to Mecca) from duties to others (*muamalat,* or social transactions or relations). But the distinction between Shariʿah (divine law) and fiqh (human interpretation and application) is the more fundamental. It underscores the extent to which much of Islamic law—from forms of government, notions of governance, to individual and collective rights and gender relations—may be seen as reflecting time-bound, human interpretations that are open to adaptation and change.

A cross section of Muslim thinkers, religious leaders, and mainstream Islamic movements from Egypt to Indonesia, Europe to America, engage in this kind of reformist interpretation of Islam and its relationship to democracy, pluralism and human rights. They include such religious scholars as Yusuf al-Qaradawi, lay scholars—Indonesia's Nurcholish Madjid, America's Abdulaziz Sachedina, and Khaled Abou El Fadl—and leaders of Islamic movements and political parties—Tunisia's Rashid al-Ghannoushi and Abdullah Gul, the prime minister of Turkey. Abdurrahman Wahid, former leader of Indonesia's Nahdatul Ulama (with some 30 million members, perhaps the largest Islamic organization in the world) and the first democratically elected president of Indonesia, is a noteworthy example.

Wahid has argued that Muslims face two choices or paths: to pursue a traditional, static, and legal-formalistic Islam or to fashion a more dynamic cosmopolitan, universal, and pluralistic worldview. In contrast to many "fundamentalists," he rejects the notion that Islam should form the basis for the nation-state's political or legal system, which he characterizes as a Middle Eastern tradition, alien to Indonesia. Indonesian Muslims should apply a moderate, tolerant brand of Islam to their daily lives in a society where "a Muslim and a non-Muslim are the same"[4]—a state in which religion and politics are separate. Rejecting legal formalism or fundamentalism as an aberration and a major obstacle to contemporary Islamic reform, Wahid has spent most of his life promoting the development of a multifaceted Muslim identity and a dynamic Islamic tradition capable of responding to the realities of modern life. Its cornerstones are free will and the right of all Muslims, both laity and religious scholars (ulema), to "perpetual reinterpretation" (ijtihad) of the Qur'an and tradition of the Prophet in light of "ever changing human situations."[5]

As in the case of other traditions—and certainly in the modern history of Roman Catholicism—reformers are often initially perceived and received as a threat by religious institutions and more conservative religious leaders and believers. In Roman Catholicism in the twentieth century, theologians were silenced or removed from their teaching positions, their careers and livelihoods threatened. Muslim reformers often find themselves in similar or worse situations—stuck between authoritarian regimes that imprison and repress and religious extremists who kill to silence voices of reform.

However, the most important challenge for Islamic reformers will be the transfer of their reformulations from the elite few to the institutions and peoples of Islam. Training the next generation of religious scholars and leaders and the laity requires institutional change, in particular curricular reforms in seminaries (madrasas), universities, and schools. As in all faiths, the religious understanding of the vast majority of believers is initially learned at home and at the local mosque, from parents and local religious leaders and teachers. Hence the importance of training those who preach and teach.

NOTES

1. Anthony Shadid, "Islamist Political Gains Test for Us," *Boston Globe,* 11 November 2002.

2. *Mideast Mirror,* 30 March 1992.

3. Abdelwahab El-Affendi, *Islam* 21 (October 2000).

4. *Business Times* (Singapore), 24 March 1999.

5. Abdurrahman Walid, "Reflections on the Need for a Concept of Man in Islam," Memorandum to the rector of the UN University, 1 May 1983, p. 3.

ISLAM IS NOT THE PROBLEM

William B. Quandt

The Bush administration, as it proceeds with its grand strategy of reordering the Middle East, talks optimistically of bringing democracy and peace to a region that has known little of either. One wonders if those who put forward this vision really believe in it, or whether they hope it will convince Americans that the war against Iraq is moral. It is puzzling that many intellectuals who have been most influential in instructing the Bush crowd on the Middle East have maintained that there is something in Arab and Islamic culture that is profoundly hostile to democracy.

The issue of Islam and democracy, so thoughtfully explored by Khaled Abou El Fadl, is both timely and important; especially significant is his focus on the doctrinal/philosophical compatibility of Islam with notions of popular sovereignty. It is worth noting that many Islamic activists would agree that Islam and democracy are incompatible. They would argue that the point in Islam is that a just ruler should uphold God's law, not that he (or she) should be popularly chosen. Indeed, insofar as there is a substantial body of Islamic political theory, it focuses on the moral dimensions of governance, not institutions and procedures, which are at the heart of modern democratic theory.

Muslim scholars like Abou El Fadl and, from a Shi'ite perspective, Abdulaziz Sachedina are impressive in demonstrating that the Qur'an and traditions can be understood in ways that are compatible with democracy—that God's sovereignty does not preclude human agency. The key issue, in their view, is that God's law involving matters of faith should not be subject to the state's intervention, that this is between God and each believer. No human being should intervene between God and a believer or pretend to judge in God's place whether the believer is sincere or not. The Qur'an specifically states that there should be no compulsion in matters of religion.

The state, however, does have a role in ordering relations among human beings so that there can be order and justice. These man-made laws should be consistent with principles of Islam, but they are understood to be products of human deliberation, hence they are fallible and therefore changeable. Nothing in Islam, according to the modernist interpretation, goes against making these laws in accordance with the notion of popular sovereignty.

These views, it should be noted, are not universally shared by Muslims, and many traditionalists would not be convinced. They fear that if too much weight is given to public opinion, then division, innovation, and disorder would result. They take seriously the Qur'anic injunction for a good Muslim to command the good and prohibit the forbidden. For centuries, Muslim rulers, and the clergy on their payrolls, have warned that the great danger to the community was disorder, or fitna, and that a strong government, provided it upheld Islamic law, was needed to prevent it. That argument is still heard in many capitals of the Arab and Islamic world and serves as a convenient justification for dictatorship.

My view of Islam and democracy starts from a different angle—
not surprisingly, since I am not a Muslim. I agree with Abou El Fadl
that Islamic doctrine and philosophy—I would broaden that to
include Islamic culture—do not preclude democracy. Every religious tradition has struggled with issues of faith and governance,
and democracy has taken root in a remarkable variety of milieus
that might seem poorly suited to nurturing it. The Qur'an per se
is not an impediment to democracy, but something does seem to
stand in the way of democratization in much of the Muslim world.

If Islam as a religion does not account for the dearth of democracies in the Muslim world, what does? To answer this we have to
look at a number of simple facts. Until about two hundred fifty
years ago, nowhere in the world was there anything resembling a
modern liberal democracy. Until then, one might argue, no culture or religion had shown itself to be compatible with the dic-
tates of democracy. Even early American democracy would get
low marks by contemporary standards, since there was no en-
franchisement for the majority of the population. Still, something
happened in the West that made it possible for a liberal form of
democracy to become the prevailing political norm today, and it
is a truly remarkable phenomenon. Can it be replicated in the
world of Islam?

We should note that the picture in the Islamic world with re-
spect to democracy is not entirely bleak. Turkey, once the heart of
Islamic orthodoxy, is a recognizable, if imperfect, democracy.
Other examples of partial democratization, including relatively
free elections, can also be noted—especially in Bangladesh and
Indonesia, two of the largest Muslim countries. And Muslims in
India regularly participate in democratic politics. Even in Jordan,
Morocco, Yemen, and Algeria embryonic democratic experiments

are under way. Iran, the most avowedly "Islamic" state in the Middle East, shows signs of democratization from the bottom up. So the landscape is not as grim as the "What Went Wrong?" school maintains. Still, there is a democratic deficit in the Islamic world compared with, say, Latin America.

As a political scientist, I suggest three strong hypotheses for the lack of democracy in the area. One has to do with the persistence of ruling monarchies in the area. Nowhere else are so many kings still wielding real power. When leadership is inherited, a core principle of democracy is sacrificed. Some of these monarchies have been overthrown—Egypt in 1952, Libya in 1969, and Iran in 1979. But a remarkable number remain intact—Morocco, Jordan, Saudi Arabia, and all the small Gulf countries. These systems are, by their nature, resistant to full democratization, although some measures of liberalization are now taking place.

Second, many of the states of the Middle East gained their independence from colonial rule after World War II and quickly adopted a then-popular model for consolidating power—the one-party populist state (with real power lodged in the military and the bureaucracy). This was supposed to provide a guarantee against instability and possible civil war, protection from the designs of neocolonialism, and a means of controlling national wealth and channeling it toward the basic needs of the people. Egypt, Syria, Algeria, and Iraq all adopted one variant or another of this model. The result has been a very durable form of authoritarianism.

Third, one of the reasons for the persistence of both monarchies and dictatorships has been the substantial oil revenues that flow directly into state coffers. This has given the states the chance to develop vast patronage networks and the upper hand in bargaining over "who gets what, when, and how," the classic issues of politics. Rentier theory does not explain everything in the Middle East, but it would be a mistake to ignore the impact of oil rents on the persistence of the prevailing economic and political order.

In conclusion, let me return to the Bush advisers who may or may not be taking democracy seriously as they make their plans for a new Middle East. First, as Abou El Fadl and others have argued, there is no reason to believe that Muslims are doctrinally unsuited for democracy. Second, a substantial constituency already favors democratic change in many Muslim countries, and many experiments are under way that merit attention. Third, external intervention is an unlikely means for advancing democracy. American efforts to this end will be viewed with great suspicion, as were those of the British and French colonialists of an earlier era. While we as Americans have every reason to hope for movement toward democracy in the Middle East, we should also be wary of those who tell us, with excessive optimism and no small dose of hubris, that democracy will readily be brought to the region by tanks and smart weapons.

Reply

KHALED ABOU EL FADL

I agree with Nader Hashemi's pertinent remark that in many ways "[t]he real focus should be not on what Islam is but rather on what Muslims want." In this valuable group of responses, I admire the fact that my non-Muslim interlocutors, John Esposito, William Quandt, Bernard Haykel, Jeremy Waldron, Noah Feldman, David Novak, and Kevin Reinhart, are respectful of the right of Muslims to direct the ethical compass of their faith and to shape their moral destinies. Unlike some other Western writers, my non-Muslim interlocutors do not assume that Muslims are fated to suffer the indignity of despotism, and they are willing to believe and respect the wishes of Muslims when they say they long for a democratic order that is consistent with their religious convictions and aspirations. Speaking as one of those Muslims who is offended by despotism and who longs for democracy, my primary purpose in this essay is to ground and anchor these aspirations into the very fabric of Islamic law and theology.

DEMOCRACY AS A MUSLIM CHOICE

In this context, Kevin Reinhart, Saba Mahmood, and others appropriately remind us of the crucial significance of context, and of the fact that socioeconomic forces often play a dominant role in shaping belief and thought. To the extent that their argument reflects a sense of cynicism about the usefulness of doctrinal arguments and their inspirational and motivational role, I disagree.

I believe that ideas, aspirations, and doctrine inspire and move people, and this is as much a part of the "practical" affairs of human existence as any other factor that causes individuals, anchored in their social settings as they are, to think, feel, and undertake particular courses of action. As Jeremy Waldron's thoughtful essay reminds us, ideas have been one of the powerful forces shaping history. It is not only that human beings are moved by ideas and thought but also that perceptions, and the way physical experiences are comprehended and interpreted, define what people will consider a material reality in the first place. Material reality cannot exist outside the realm of thoughts, ideas, and convictions, which includes firmly held religious or ideological beliefs. Religious convictions, among others, affect the way reality is defined and comprehended. Furthermore, religion is among the most powerful forces affecting human determinations, choices, and all possible courses of behavior.

Some writers and scholars insist on ignoring the role of religious conviction in the lives of believing Muslims and wishfully proclaim that theology and theological debates do not matter. But these writers do not describe a sociological reality of which they objectively take note and at the same time do not wish to influence or judge. Rather, in my view, these writers project onto their subjects of study their own convictions and preferences while ignoring the fact that for numerous individuals, including myself, God is an ever-present reality and that, for them, religion is an essential frame of reference for all normative judgments. The skepticism many writers voiced about the role of theology is often the by-product of the inability, or unwillingness, of these authors to understand the often powerful and decisive role that a passion about God can play in the construction of perceptions of reality and in defining the choices made when confronted by the possibilities of the future.

MUSLIMS AND THE WESTERN DEMOCRATIC EXPERIENCE

If Muslims become convinced that democracy, with its concomitant commitments in favor of constitutionalism, the rule of law, and civil and political rights, is not only desirable but also an Islamic imperative, at least they will commence the process of overcoming any context-based challenges that confront them. For Muslims who are committed to the teachings of the Qur'an and the Prophet and who are influenced by the interpretive communities of the past, a democratic commitment cannot be made in a doctrinal vacuum. Such a commitment will necessarily be made in reference to, and in reconciliation with, their religious convictions and understandings. In this process of reconciliation, I do not at all exclude the possibility that in light of the Western experience, democratic theory and practice may have to be modified, or even improved upon. Furthermore, I fully agree with Waldron that Muslims do not have to imitate the steps undertaken by Christian thought over the past five hundred years. But it is necessary to consider and learn from the failures and successes of non-Muslims, especially the democratic West. As Waldron notes, Muslims have played a significant role in sponsoring the intellectual development of the West. And, contrary to the dogmatic claims of cultural relativists and purists, it is important to remember that powerful humanitarian ideas enjoy a mixed lineage, and this lineage has much Muslim blood. I fear that the willingness of some to assume that there is an inextricable convergence between the moral assumptions at the heart and core of a democratic system and the West betrays a cultural centrism that tends to void universal human values. While the West might appropriately claim the pride of authorship over the institutional and procedural system that we call democracy, this does not mean that the moral and ethical val-

ues that inform such a system are exclusively Western in origin or
nature. For example, Umar Ibn al-Khattab, the Second Caliph and
Companion of the Prophet, is reported to have chided a governor
for overreaching his authority by saying: "Who has permitted you
to treat people like slaves when they were born free!" In addition,
in a statement that is characteristic of the Qur'anic ethical outlook,
the Qur'an proclaims: "Hold to forgiveness [as a way of life], promote that which is known to people to be good, and keep away
from the ignorant" (7:199). Freedom, forgiveness and tolerance,
and the pursuit of overlapping consensual ethical commitments
are virtues that are important for a democracy, but they are not exclusively Western.

I am mindful of the cautious warnings by some of this book's
essayists against an uncritical idealization of the Western liberal
democratic experience. But I do think that John Esposito gets it
exactly right when he asserts that reformist efforts at democratization "do not imply uncritical acceptance of Western democratic forms." As I emphasized in my essay, democracy is a moral
and ideological institution that is to be sought after out of a normative commitment. The possibility that the West, or for that matter any other cultural and sociopolitical unit, failed to live up to
the democratic ideal is something to be considered, but it does
necessarily negate the desirability of making a normative commitment, as a Muslim, in pursuit of the democratic ideal.

THE QUESTION OF ISLAMIC AUTHENTICITY

The primary focus of my essay has been Islamic doctrinal justification and reconciliation, and not the history and subtleties of
democratic theory. Nonetheless, I agree with Haykel's and Waldron's comments that democracy is not just about the rule of law

or a system of rights; it is also about the integrity of process and the practice of legitimate opposition. But in my view, these are instrumentalities that make a democracy meaningful and that ensure the survival of the system. At the core of democracy are the ideas of representative government, limits on the power of government, and the safeguarding of basic and fundamental human rights. There are derivative but necessary rights and institutions that flow from this core, such as the right to associate and to form oppositional groups, the right to reflect and think and to attempt to convince others of one's ideas, and the importance of an independent and fair judiciary. As to Islamic doctrine, I think that once the core beliefs of a democracy are reconciled, the particulars and derivations become much easier to justify as important and necessary to the more fundamental commitment to the principle of democratic governance. Even at the intellectual and doctrinal level, working out the full details is a long-term and complex process that can only commence if, in principle, the democratic commitment is explicitly and honestly addressed. This is the primary purpose of my essay.

In this context, it is worth emphasizing that my theological argument draws on six basic ideas: (1) human beings are God's vicegerents and deputies on earth; (2) this relationship of vicegerency is the basis of individual and personal responsibility; (3) this individual responsibility and vicegerency is also the basis for human rights and equality; (4) human beings in general, and Muslims more specifically, have the fundamental obligation to foster justice (and more generally to command right and forbid wrong) and to preserve and promote God's creation; (5) there is a basic and fundamental distinction between the divine law and fallible human interpretations; and (6) the state should not pretend to embody or represent the divine sovereignty and majesty.

This summary in itself provides a sufficient response to many of the misplaced criticisms proffered by Mohammad Fadel and Muqtedar Khan. I agree with Fadel that only time will tell whether my specific doctrinal arguments will convince the majority or at least a sizable portion of Muslims. But I most definitely would challenge Fadel's apparent speculative conviction that he represents a greater measure of orthodoxy or legitimacy. More to the point, however, is Fadel's methodology of claiming to work from the bottom up. Instead of formulating and admitting moral and normative commitments that are informed and inspired by the interpretive efforts of the past and then investigating the corollary and necessary implications of these a priori commitments, Fadel would rather approach the Islamic doctrinal tradition with a blank page, so to speak, and then discover the imperatives and mandates of the tradition. In sum, Fadel apparently thinks he can investigate the divine will in its unadulterated and pristine form.

Both Fadel and I consult the tradition and do not dismiss it as a historical irrelevancy. Both he and I seem to recognize that the texts of the past are contextually bound and contingent, but both of us realize that we ought to learn from the efforts, struggles, successes, and failures of those who preceded us and from their intellectual and moral legacy. Furthermore, apparently both of us believe that most Muslims would rather live in a political system that guarantees and respects their rights and dignity, and that most Muslims would regard despotism as unjust, oppressive, and morally offensive. But Fadel seems to think that he can rid himself of his own bonded and contingent context and subjectivities as he uncovers the objective moral and normative trajectory of the Islamic tradition. Very inconsistently, he is willing to proclaim, in a language that imitates judicial certitude, the rationalist (Mu'tazali), Aristotelian, and Neoplatonist traditions within Islam

as representing a "heretofore discredited theological argument."
This only begs a whole set of questions: When and who, exactly,
proclaimed these trajectories as discredited? Ash'ari Islam, Salafi
Islam, Wahhabi Islam, neo-Wahhabi Islam, the majority of Muslim
jurists across the ages, the Muslim masses, Fadel, or God?

THE AUTHORITY TO DEFINE ISLAM

These questions serve to highlight the more fundamental problem
of who and what is the basis of authority in Islam. David Novak's
valuable contribution demonstrates that challenges pertaining to
the authority, or authoritativeness, of reason and the role to be
played by human subjectivities and contextually contingent experiences, in light of the revealed law, are not unique to the Islamic
tradition. Like Novak, I do not believe that pure reason standing
alone creates or defines what is good and moral or that the law of
God should be subordinated to human autonomy. I fully agree
with Novak that justice, as philosophically formulated, informs,
but does not ground, the interpretation and application of the revealed law. Most of all, as Novak perceptively points out, divine authority and human authority are needed in a system that achieves
justice through the revealed law while avoiding the distortions of
oligarchies, whether clerical or secular. Moreover, Novak is right
on point when he asserts that there exist universal norms of justice that do not in any way negate the sanctity of the revealed law,
and that, in fact, are more intensely and, in my view, perfectly fulfilled by the divine law. In my opinion, the perception and comprehension of universals, such as goodness, morality, and beauty
(*husn*), are improved and refined in an interactive and dialectical
dynamic between revelation and human reflection upon nature
and creation, as well as human understandings of their own

sociohistorical experiences. In this dialectical process of comprehension, I distinguish between structural readings of the text, especially the Qur'an, and the reading of discrete and particular passages such as the passage on the punishment for theft. In doing so, the structural moral compass and direction to beauty and goodness (for instance, the command to seek justice, mercy, compassion, honesty, and modesty) are provided by human engagement with revelation—an engagement where revelation plays the role of teacher and educator, but the students (that is, human beings) are not expected to relinquish their intuitive, emotional, and rational faculties in this educative process. In this outlook, human beings are expected to admit, reflect, and at times discipline their subjectivities as they are guided by their understanding of the divine nature and will, but their subjectivities and personal experiences are not treated as irrelevant or offensive. And, most significantly for me, especially when it comes to the discrete and particular, human beings ought not indulge in the pretense of being privy to and perfectly aware of the divine will. Per this outlook, human beings, and especially Muslim scholars and jurists, in discharging their duties and obligations of vicegerency, should aid the integrity, honesty, and transparency of the process by at least making a real effort to openly acknowledge and admit their own subjectivities, ethical reflections, and normative commitments.

Fadel himself demonstrates the pitfalls of a methodology that is insufficiently cognizant of its own context and that is inadequately sensitized to its own subjectivities. After deciding that the rationalist argument is discredited, Fadel proclaims that the ultimate good in Islam is salvation, and not justice. In the first place, in my view, the emphasis on salvation instead of justice, or for that matter peace, mercy, compassion, forgiveness, repentance, truth, or even submission and obedience, reflects the impact of Christian symbolism and language. In Qur'anic Arabic, there is no literal equivalent to the word *salvation;* even more, I would argue that an analysis of the Qur'anic text would demonstrate that the concept of salvation, as it exists in the Christian theological tradition, is foreign to both the language and spirit of the Qur'an. In addition, I would distinguish between the Qur'anic discourse on reward and punishment, heaven and hellfire, forgiveness, repentance, peace, the straight path, and the struggle in the way of God from the very concepts of absolution and salvation. Moreover, I would argue that doing good, struggling to enjoin the good and forbid the evil, and being just with oneself and other human beings and creation are part and parcel of finding the balance (*al-mizan*), equanimity, and peace. I would further argue that the pursuit of this peace, balance, and justice is at the core of the submission to God and the obligations of vicegerency. My point here is that every part of my context—my intellectual upbringing, personal history, and theological training—lead me to find Fadel's claims about salvation foreign and odd.

Second—and here again I note the highly context-based nature of Fadel's assertions—Fadel's comments about law reflect the influence of the American legal context on his thinking. Fadel is an American lawyer by training and is currently in practice, and quite understandably he enriches his understanding of Islamic law by drawing on the conceptual categories derived from the American legal tradition. A case in point is Fadel's distinction between substantive and procedural justice—what he claims is in the Qur'anic terms *ʿadl* and *maʿruf.* Since Fadel claims to work from the bottom up, I wonder where in the Islamic legal or exegetical tradition he finds the differentiation between procedural and substantive due process. To my knowledge, no theologian or jurist ever equated the Qur'anic term *ʿadl* with substantive justice and

ʿurf with procedural justice. In fact, limiting the term *ʿurf,* which means what is customarily and socially accepted as right and good, to procedural justice strikes me as odd and unsupported. While I do agree that there are antecedents in the interpretive tradition—whether in the writings of al-Qarafi or of others—which can be interpreted to support a differentiation between substantive and procedural justice in the modern context, the fact remains that Fadel projects the contextual constructs and formulations of the American legal tradition on Qur'anic exegeses and the understanding of the legacy of Islamic law. This in itself is not objectionable. Enriching the Islamic discourse methodologically with the diverse subjective experiences and contextual understandings of various participants can be desirable—in part because it is a necessary step toward utilizing the full richness of God's creation. It is troubling, however, when interpreters are oblivious to their own limitations or context. This obliviousness is rendered more problematic when interpreters, like Fadel, claim that "revelation, whether Qur'anic or . . . Prophetic sayings, has always been deemed to be a model of literary excellence and clarity[,]" in order to conceal or obfuscate their own contingencies and subjectivities. Interestingly, Fadel's own attempt at Qur'anic exegesis belies his largely rhetorical claim about the purported clarity of the text.

As to Fadel's substantive argument about what might or might not be considered American law, he misses the point. I realize that my argument regarding the state and its relationship to Shariʿa is most controversial, and at present it might not convince the majority of Muslims. But as I argued in my essay, I believe that it is epistemologically, theologically, and politically necessary in order to safeguard the Shariʿa and the state from failure or abuse. The American example might lend more support to my approach than Fadel realizes. There is an ideal, encapsulated in the notions of the inherent, natural, and inalienable, that guides and inspires the investigations and lawmaking efforts of the legal system in the United States. Whether we label that inspiring ideal the will of the founding fathers, the penumbra of the Constitution, the gloss of the Constitution, the compelling and natural interests, the preemptive norms, *jus cogens* (an international law concept), or even simply common sense, the judiciary and legislature undertake their legalistic activities in the light of the fundamental values honored and respected by our foundational and basic laws. In fact, the legislature can pass a law (for instance, the PATRIOT Act), and the courts reach judgments (for instance, the *Korematsu* decision), and yet the sociohistorical judgment could be, and often is, that these legal determinations do not represent what is genuinely reflective of either America or its jurisprudential system. There is an endless and indefatigable process of exploration and self-definition in which in one sense all of our legal determinations are American, and in many other senses very few of these determinations will become irreversibly associated with the true identity and nature of America. Of course, there is an aspirational fiction at play here, but it is necessary to maintaining the integrity and purity of the national ideal. What Fadel ignores is that when it comes to honoring the immutable divine ideal, the need for this approach becomes all the more compelling.

THE DIFFERENCE AMONG ISLAMICISTS

Although I believe that my argument is firmly anchored in the Islamic tradition and I remain hopeful that this argument will eventually become accepted orthodoxy within the Islamic world, my awareness of its current controversial nature brings me to a problematic claim made by Feldman in his response. Feldman seems to think that there is no substantial difference between my position and argument and the positions of other Islamicists such as Rashid al-Ghannouchi, Yusuf al-Qaradawi, or Fahmi Huwaidi. Although Feldman admits that these thinkers "disagree on a wide range of issues," he goes on to indicate certain points of overlap. However, in emphasizing points of agreement (which surely exist), Feldman obscures fundamental points of disagreement, which go to the heart of my argument. Unlike, for instance, Huwaidi, and also unlike many Muslim reformers like Khan, I do not first pretend that Islam invented democracy before anyone else and then proceed to essentialize the doctrinal sources and the early Islamic experience into a one-dimensional narrative in pursuit of democracy. I also do not pretend to be privy to the divine will and then claim to discover that the truth of the Islamic revelation is really all about democracy. Huwaidi's and Qaradawi's proclamations on democracy are dogmatic at best; they do not exhibit any serious understanding of the doctrinal challenges a democracy poses for traditional understandings of Islam. As a result, both writers speak about Islam and democracy only in the most vague and general sense, without engaging the particulars of history or doctrine. In essence, showing the place of democratic values within Islam is a more demanding interpretive task than these authors are willing or able to acknowledge. Even more, all three authors mentioned by Feldman espouse the establishment of an Islamic state, which rules in God's name and enforces Shariʿah law as the will of both God and the state. I do not believe in such a state, and even more, I consider such a state a form of idolatry. Moreover, all three authors do not assign the same importance to basic individual rights that I do. These authors fail to make the same type of commitment to individual rights as inherent and fundamental rights that are held against society and the state.

What is of particular concern for me here is the tendency of both Western scholars of Islam and Muslim apologists not to pay much attention to the details and particularities of the arguments made from the vantage point of Muslim theology and law. I am not accusing Feldman, who is usually a careful researcher, of being one of those generalizing scholars. The point that I suspect Feldman would agree with is that especially when dealing with theology and law, the microdiscourses and the details do matter. For example, although Huwaidi, like many other Muslim and non-Muslim writers, is quite comfortable with making sweeping generalizations about the real character and nature of the Islamic theological and legal tradition, his competence and knowledge of the tradition that he attempts to characterize is seriously in question. In the same way, while Qaradawi has mastered the Islamic tradition, he only has the most superficial and casual knowledge of the institutions and theories of democracy. As a result, in his writings, Qaradawi treats democracy basically as an institution that gives effect to the will of the majority. Since Qaradawi assumes that the majority of the citizenry of an Islamic state will be Muslim, he does not foresee any problems with applying Shariʿah law in a democratic state. As argued earlier, the idea of a democratic state governed by divine law is highly problematic. The important point here is that as we seek to understand, evaluate, and engage Muslim debates, it is imperative that we pay attention to who is saying exactly what and that we focus on the evidentiary quality of the arguments. In my view, the lineage or sociocultural identity of the arguments are not nearly as important as their persuasive and evidentiary quality.

LIBERAL MUSLIMS AND THE PLIGHT
OF THE ISLAMIC TRADITION

On the issue of competence over the doctrinal and interpretive tradition, I reserve my most emphatic disagreements for the article by Khan. Interestingly, while Feldman worries that I might be going too far in meeting the necessary conditions for a democracy by diluting Shariʿah, Khan writes that I do not go far enough. Khan thinks that Muslims should forget about Shariʿah altogether in order to be entirely free to pursue philosophy, political theory, or simple utilitarian interest. Otherwise, he warns that I, and Muslims who agree with me, are doomed to perpetuate a Khomeini-style theocracy, where jurists (*fuqaha*) become the representative of the divine will and truth. Khan does not engage my specific arguments, but he seems confident that the mere specter of Shariʿah is sufficient to derail the quest for democracy. Like the liberal Jewish reformers, who Novak warns were not very good for the Jewish tradition, Khan believes that Shariʿah should be either whatever Muslims wish it to be or subordinated to everything else, including common sense, logic, human experience, social and political aspirations, and the will of the majority.

Khan, however, does not dismiss all of the Islamic doctrinal sources and history as irrelevant. Rather, he selectively focuses on the precedent of the so-called Constitution of Medina, which he anachronistically reinvents as a social contract that did not impose Islamic law on anyone. In Khan's creative reconstruction of early Islamic history and thought, either there are no specialized Muslim jurists or every Muslim, by virtue of being a Muslim, becomes a jurist.

In my view, Khan's rhetoric perfectly exemplifies the problem with much of the contemporary work done by Islamist reformers. Muslims who are not willing to consider this reinvented and

largely ahistorical construction of the so-called Constitution of
Medina as the only relevant historical precedent, and who are
aware of the many other Qur'anic and Prophetic precedents that
make Shari'ah central to a Muslim's life, respond in an equally dismissive fashion to Khan's claims. In fact, Muslim postcolonial intellectual history has been, for the most part, trapped between the
opposite poles of those who show little or no regard for the efforts of the interpretive communities of the past and those who
exhibit a slavish adherence to these communities. In the process,
a serious and analytically rigorous discourse on Islam and democracy is yet to develop. As to these reformers, their methodology, or
in reality the absence of one, often poses insurmountable obstacles to the possibility of engaging them in a systematic fashion.
Shari'ah, which in Islamic theology is identified as the way to the
fulfillment of the divine will, has enjoyed a revered position in the
Islamic tradition. The processes of Shari'ah search the divine will
by reference to doctrinal and historical sources, such as the
Qur'an, the statements of the Prophet, and the precedent of the
Companions of the Prophet, as well as utilizing a variety of rational or sociological devices (such as studying human custom
and considering public interest). Although some reformers, like
Khan, rebel against the prized position of Shari'ah, they rarely explore the implications of their positions upon Islamic theology or
even revelation. For instance, does the dismissal of Shari'ah mean
that God has no will as to human beings? Is the will of God contingent and dependent on the will of the Muslim majority? If so,
why? Does the dismissal of Shari'ah mean the abrogation of all the
rituals of Islam, which, after all, are part of Shari'ah? Does this
mean that the Qur'anic commandments and the historical reports
about the Prophet's conduct and statements become irrelevant?
Are some relevant but not others, and according to which criteria?

The type of undisciplined selectiveness that is characteristic of liberal reformers does serious violence to the traditions of Islam without replacing them with anything coherent or meaningful. In hoping to achieve democratic egalitarianism, Khan and others end up discarding the determinations of the interpretive communities of the past and Islamic law itself. Such reformers also end up diluting the distinctiveness and particularity of Islam and replacing it with a stark form of unprincipled functionalism. The Qur'an itself, however, challenges Khan's extreme form of egalitarianism when it commands some members of society to specialize in the study of the will of God and instructs Muslims to seek the guidance of those specialized people when necessary (see 9:122, 16:43). In democratizing ijtihad (the independent exercise of judgment about a point of law), however, reformers like Khan effectively vest every Muslim, and perhaps every non-Muslim, regardless of age, education, rationality, or piety, with the competence to be a jurist. Assuming that this so-called lay and naturally endowed jurist will seek to convince others of the legitimacy of his or her contentions about Islam, and that he or she might even ask for deference from others to his or her determinations and judgments, this only begs the question, On what basis and according to what criteria should Muslims evaluate the juristic determinations of this person? Even more, Khan, like many other liberal reformers, invokes the doctrine of ijtihad without any regard for the fact that this very concept was produced and developed by the juristic interpretive communities of the past. Khan fails to explain his criteria for selectively utilizing a concept generated by the interpretive communities of the past but then stripping it of all inherited meanings. It is difficult to imagine the basis for issuing authoritative opinions and *fatawa* (*responsa*) about revelation and the will of God when the only qualification, according to Khan, is the ability to speak, and perhaps write, and a medium for delivery (such as a podium or the Internet).

Since the onslaught of colonialism and modernity, the condition and very status of the Islamic intellectual and legal traditions have been in a state of intense instability and flux. The fortunes of this Islamic legacy, with its numerous orientations and trajectories, have wavered between those who have grabbed on to it as a defensive mechanism against the powerful forces of modernity and those who have sought to liberate themselves entirely of the past by surrendering themselves to their modern context without much regard for the insights and wisdom of past generations. The very education of Muslim intellectuals has tended to sharpen this polarization. Muslim intellectuals either have been educated in the intellectual heritage and the interpretive communities of modernity, which usually has meant the thought of the West, or have been educated and gained competence in the Islamic interpretive communities of the precolonial past.

RESISTANCE AND THE REJECTION OF THE WEST

This brings me to a final point raised by several of my interlocutors. Several of the essayists in this book argued for what may be called the epistemological fairness criticism. In their enthusiasm to be epistemologically fair and to be respectful of the integrity of the Islamic experience, they expressed much skepticism about the universality of Western values. Fadel, for instance, poses Islam, as he imagines it, as representing an alternative to the failures of the West. Mahmood warns against assuming that the Western experience is the standard according to which the rest of humanity is to be measured or evaluated. As noted earlier, I agree with this cautious stand, but I worry that by insisting on preserving the

avowed distinctiveness and particularity of Islam, we end up ab-
rogating and voiding the universality of the Islamic experience. I
also worry that we will unwittingly end up transforming Islam
into a marginal eccentricity. By seeking to protect Islam from the
imperialistic Western universalisms, many scholars end up run-
ning the risk of deconstructing and marginalizing Islam as a central player in a shared human moral legacy. For a long time, one of
the basic criticisms leveled against the Orientalist legacy has been
that it inflicts on Islam, as a sociohistorical tradition and a normative symbolic construct, an alienism, exoticism, and esotericism
and projects on Islam the fears, insecurities, and imperialist fan-
tasies of the Orientalist scholars themselves. The irony, however,
is that although the very impetus, and indeed the very raison
d'être, for the critical scholarly agenda of many writers espousing
epistemological fairness has been to undo the legacy of colonialism and Orientalism, the concrete impact of their work has not
been very different from the legacy that they seek to challenge
and undo.

For writers like Mahmood and Fadel, Islam has become the
symbolic platform for their subjective protestations and resistance against the power of Western epistemology in the post-
modern condition. But although they espouse cultural relativism
and deconstruct the validity of Western universalisms, Mahmood
and Fadel offer no moral alternatives. More seriously, they also
dilute the very notion of fundamental and basic humanitarian values. For instance, Mahmood warns against the unthinking acceptance of Western paradigms of individual rights and contends that
Muslim societies might value collective social rights over individual rights. However, he ignores the fact that the language of
collective social rights has been persistently exploited by the governments of Muslim countries to suppress dissent and strengthen

the state at the expense of its citizens. Furthermore, it is fair to say that to date no democracy has managed to survive while founding itself on a bed of collective rights. Mahmood does not explain how she proposes to get beyond the historical practice that, for the purpose of establishing democracies, clearly favors the paradigm of individual rights. In fact, the historical practice of democracies seems compelling because it is the individual who needs the greatest protection against the state and society. Mahmood's deference to collective rights might be anthropologically more genuine or authentic in some situations. But there is no reason to believe that such deference is more genuine or authentic from the perspective of either democracy or Islamic theology, both of which emphasize individual accountability and reward, and which honor and dignify each person as the bearer of duties and rights.

GETTING BEYOND REACTIVE THINKING
AND THE PURSUIT OF DEMOCRACY

Mahmood's and Fadel's criticisms point to a much more basic problem—that of the highly reactive and politicized condition of modern Muslim discourses. Much of the Islamic discourse is captive to the historical experience of colonialism as well as the reality of contemporary imperialism, and so it is held hostage to a traumatized condition in which there is an intense concern for autonomy and liberation; but it is also coupled with an oblivious disregard of the need for self-definition. In many ways, the problem is that confronted with the often gruesome political realities of the Muslim world, one is seriously tempted to surrender to a deep sense of cynicism about the claims of democracy, freedom, and dignity for all. But the abusive use of moral universals to justify immoral conduct ought not dissuade anyone from recognizing the worthiness and desirability of a political system that tends to limit the abusive use of power and augments the protections afforded to individuals so that they can discharge their obligations as God's vicegerents without being at the mercy of despots.

In conclusion, I believe that if democracy is to become a systematic normative goal of large numbers of Muslims in Muslim countries, it will have to be anchored in both Islam and modernity. To achieve this objective, a serious discourse that negotiates between, but does not dismiss, the past and the present and that negotiates between slavish imitation and unprincipled and self-indulgent inventiveness is imperative. This is exactly what makes the engagements between my interlocutors and me particularly valuable. The fact that this civil debate is taking place while the coercion and oppressiveness of terrorism, invasions, and war are galvanizing the attention of the world only serves to emphasize the crucial need for a greater respect for human rights and the democratic practice of civil discourse.

CONTRIBUTORS

KHALED ABOU EL FADL is Visiting Professor of Law at Yale Law School and Professor of Law at the UCLA School of Law. He serves on the U.S. Commission on International Religious Freedom, and is a member of the Board of Directors of Human Rights Watch. He is both an Islamic jurist and American lawyer, and is the author of six books and numerous articles on Islamic law. His latest book is *The Place of Tolerance in Islam.*

JOHN L. ESPOSITO, University Professor and professor of religion and international affairs at Georgetown University, is the author of *Unholy War: Terror in the Name of Islam* and *Islam and Democracy* (with John Voll).

MOHAMMAD H. FADEL has clerked on the United States Court of Appeals for the Fourth Circuit and currently practices law in Manhattan. In addition, he has a Ph.D. in Near Eastern Languages and Civilizations and has published several articles on Islamic law.

NOAH FELDMAN, assistant professor of law at the New York University School of Law, is the author of *After Jihad.*

NADER A. HASHEMI is a doctoral candidate in the Department of Political Science at the University of Toronto. He is completing a dissertation entitled "Toward a Democratic Theory for Muslim Societies: Rethinking the Relationship between Religion, Secularism, and Democracy."

BERNARD HAYKEL is assistant professor of Middle Eastern and Islamic studies at New York University and the author of *Revival and Reform in Islam: The Legacy of Muhammad al-Shawkani.*

SABA MAHMOOD teaches at the University of California, Berkeley. Her work focuses on issues of secularism, gender, and modernity within the context of Islamist movements in the Middle East and South Asia.

M. A. MUQTEDAR KHAN, director of international studies, assistant professor and chair of the Department of Political Science at Adrian College, is the author of *American Muslims: Bridging Faith and Freedom.*

DAVID NOVAK is the J. Richard and Dorothy Shiff Professor of Jewish Studies at the University of Toronto and is the author of *Covenantal Rights.*

WILLIAM B. QUANDT is Edward R. Stettinius Professor of Politics at the University of Virginia and the author of *Peace Process* and *Between Ballots and Bullets.*

A. KEVIN REINHART teaches Islamic and religious studies at Dartmouth College. He works on Islamic ethics and late Ottoman-period Islam.

JEREMY WALDRON is Maurice and Hilda Friedman Professor of Law at Columbia University. His most recent books are *Law and Disagreement* and *God, Locke, and Equality.*

INDEX

opposition, 112-13; popular support for, 79-80; practical impediments to, 77; and reactive thinking, 127-28; religious vs. secular justifications of, 89; and revealed law, 87-92; rights as desideratum of, 88-89, 113; rights required for, 60 (*see also* individual rights; rights); and the rule of law, 56-58, 85; spread of, 103-4; vs. theocracy, 83; Western intervention for, 52-53

democrats, Islamic, 62

despotism, 17-18, 80, 109, 127-28

dictatorships, 102, 104-5

dignity, 55, 84, 86n.1

disagreement, 43n.41, 55-58

disorder (fitna), 13, 102

dissidents, 57

diverse interests, 57-58

diversity: within Islam, 70, 95-96, 98; Muhammad on, 40n.23; the Qur'an on, 19-20, 22, 40n.23, 75; in religious traditions, 95; theological justification of, 84; and tolerance, 75

divine law vs. fallible human interpretations, 113

doctrinal vs. practical arguments, 109-10

Douglas, Mary, 70

duties to God vs. others, 98

Egypt, 39n.13, 93, 94, 104

entitlements, 83, 88-89

epistemological fairness criticism, 125-26

equality, 55, 60

Eshkavari, Hassan Yousefi, 52

Esposito, John, 109, 112

ethic of care, 40n.22

expediency laws (al-ahkam al-siyasiyyah), 14

extremists, 61-62, 93, 96

Fadel, Mohammad, 114-15, 116-18, 119, 125, 126

Fahd, king of Saudi Arabia, 96

fanaticism, 51

al-Fārābī, 61

fasting, 98

fatawa (responsa), 124-25

Feldman, Noah, 109, 119-21, 122

fiqh (human interpretation/application), 31, 44n.42, 98

fitna (disorder), 13, 102

five basic values (al-daruriyyat al-khamsah), 23-24, 27-28, 41n.27

forgiveness (maghfira), 40n.21

fornication, 24

Francis of Assisi, 95

free association, 60

freedom of conscience, 60

free speech, 60

Fuller, Graham, 54n.7

fundamentalist, modern vs. premodern, 8, 37n.3

genocidal regimes, 53

al-Ghannouchi, Rashid, 59-60, 74, 99, 119-20

al-Ghazali, Abu Hamid, 17-18, 19, 70

God: authority of vs. human authority, 88-89, 92, 115; beauty/virtue as approximations of, 22, 40-41n.24; duties to, 98; on human beings as vicegerents of, 6, 19, 21, 22-23, 37-38n.4, 89; Oneness of (tawhid), 38n.8, 96-97; political dominion of (hakimiyyat Allah), 7, 38n.5; rights